D1519877

EDUCATION IS A SHUCK

How the Educational System Is Failing Our Children

Carl Weinberg
University of California at Los Angeles
and
The Center For Humanistic Education

WILLIAM MORROW & COMPANY, INC.
NEW YORK 1975

For Lois
    Who doesn't know how to shuck

1 2 3 4 5   79 78 77 76 75

Library of Congress Catalog Card Number 74-11775

ISBN 0-688-02879-9

Preface

When I first began my career as a professional educator some fifteen years ago I was unable to see schools and schooling as if they might be otherwise. They were what they were and I was what I was; I was trying to behave appropriately within the framework of formal education as I had known it to be. I was quite successful at everything—teaching, getting graduate degrees, getting papers published, getting a professorship in a top school, even getting tenure. The only thing I was unsuccessful at was finding a way to be comfortable with who I was and what I was doing.

In those years I suffered considerable anxiety, sometimes to the point of anguish, because something deep inside kept telling me that the way I was doing things was not the way that was best for me. In all honesty, it was out of the psychological need for survival, or at least sanity, that I began to inspect the world that I came to inhabit, of schools and schooling, and to make changes in relation to my life in that world. It was not that I discovered an ideology first and began to adapt my life to it. I first knew that I had to change and had to find a place in which to change. I decided that, in the absence of a set of abstract ideas, I would try to be comfortable and build a rationale around what made me comfortable. It was not hedonism; my comfort often involved very hard work, struggle, with very few successes. Being comfortable only meant being as real as I could be, and moving as far away as I could from those rituals which robbed me of my individuality. My struggles have been my therapy. They have raised my consciousness to a point where I can no longer tolerate contradictions in which I am expected to participate. Those contradictions are the theme of this book. Only by discovering them and struggling out from under them does one become whole.

I would like to dedicate this book in general to all those who have helped me in this struggle, even though most of those to whom I refer have little or no idea that they played any part. Sometimes my leaders were those who tried to convince me that they had the answer. Other times the major contribution was made by someone who so embodied the contradiction that I had to smile at myself for not seeing it before.

And then there were those who cared enough for me to encourage me in any changes that my own life would take. Those I knew who would not be bothered by any changes whatever, as long as whatever I did made me happy, are foremost. My mother and father have been lifelong fans, and their approval has not required any specific way of being for me. My daughters Marca and Hayley are the same in their own way. As a result of my accepting them for whatever they are or will be, they are reciprocating in kind. My wife Lois goes me one better. She discovers contradictions in my anticontradiction life, and helps me to work them through.

Another person who has strongly influenced my ideas in this book is Tom Robischon, a colleague whose recent destructive firing personifies for me the most monumental contradiction of my academic environment: that there is no room for wisdom in the university. Wisdom, as I understand it, and I have thought quite a bit about it, does not pay off in the kind of rewards that the university offers. We have rules and if one doesn't play by those rules one loses the game. Wise people seldom have either the awareness or the stomach to play by those defeating rules.

Beatrice Winchell, my friend, my proofreader, my personal editor, and my typist, has done much to make this book into something of which I approve. I commend her to anyone who has something important to say but can't quite get it said in the way one would like.

A final note of gratitude to Roger Williams of Dryden press and to the men and women that he has chosen to work with the manuscript.

C. W.

Los Angeles, Calif.
April, 1973

Contents

School is a Great Big Shuck

This book is about games people play in schools and the rules by which they play. The most broadly encompassing term that I could find to describe these games is shucking. As a way of life shucking has become highly developed. Anything so important to everyday functioning must, of necessity, become refined. It is a matter of survival.

If we were classifying shucks, terms such as important or trivial, credible or incredible, overused or appropriately used, ingenious or routine would come into play. An example of an appropriately used shuck would be telling the teacher that you missed school because your grandmother died. An overused shuck would be to tell her the same thing the following month.

Sociologists call it socialization. Socialization in American society is learning how to shuck, learning how to communicate the identity that brings about the biggest and best rewards. A car salesman acts as if the car he is about to sell you is an absolute steal. The more he is able to convince you of his lie the richer he will become. School teachers and professors and students play the same game with variations that are particular to school life.

School is where we learn how to shuck. What kids really learn in school is how to succeed. Any learning (as you know) which is not directly linked to grades is defined as irrelevant. So we learn how to beat the system. And we learn it from everybody because everybody is doing it. At times, when I was teaching in the public schools, I used to think the best thing we could do for a kid is help him to pull off his shuck. For example, I had a homeroom full of marginal illiterates who, for reasons we will deal with throughout the book, were forced into delinquent patterns. They would smoke in the bathroom, steal pocketbooks, yell "mother fucker" across the room, trip kids in line, bully their way to the front of the line—just normal stuff for working class kids. I had about an 80 percent detention rate until I decided to help my boys play the shucking game.

Usually, when a kid pulls something, he isn't detected directly. A teacher or a vice principal or a student monitor might think he spotted the criminal and he would confront him as if he were sure. Usually the kid would then confess since he would think that he was caught in the act.

Anyhow, I taught my boys to say "I haven't done anything, sir," in a nice way, whereas before they would say "I ain't done nothin," in a mean way. My boys learned that if you're going to beat the system you have to sound like you're not lower class. My boys' detention rate dropped considerably.

Now, the reason shucks work is that everybody has a stake in them, the shuckers and the victims of the shuck. Another way of expressing this notion is that we let people get away with their shucking because we expect to be doing the same at some time. Also, we all seem to believe we have an investment in maintaining social relations on a stable base. We wouldn't walk into a dinner party and tell the hostess that we are sure that her house is not usually this clean. We let people put on their show for us because we put it on for them or somebody else, next time.

Shucking, it must be understood, is vastly more complex than the obvious little deceits that most people get into all the time. In the school, as well as in the larger society, the real shuck occurs when we put each other on through the conviction that we are meeting other peoples' expectations and thereby maintaining the equilibrium of socie-ty, or culture, or relationship. With this broader conception in mind we can say that a shucking event occurs when one person attempts to convince another person that he deserves either to be rewarded or to be left alone by virtue of the fact that he is doing what everybody expects of him, even though he would rather be doing something else, probably somewhere else, and probably with someone else.

There are variations in the presentation of a shuck: we have both manifest and latent forms of shucking. Manifest is when you say or do your shuck and latent is when you communicate by omission. When a teacher tells students they should follow her example, that is manifest. When kids pick up the idea that a teacher is moral because they never see her smoke or drink, or hear her curse, that is latent.

Then there is the difference between the believed shuck and the nonbelieved shuck. When a person who tells you that he is a moral man really believes it, that is the former category. When he tells you he is an honest man and he knows that he's a liar, that's a nonbelieved shuck. We get both kinds in schools. Somehow, if we are making moral judgments, it is easier to forgive a person who believes his shuck is real than it is to forgive an out and out liar or hypocrite.

Sociologists talk about real and ideal norms. This refers to the things we *say* we believe or value and the things we *really* believe and value. Some people, probably many, believe their teachers and parents when they are told what is and isn't right or important. These are the people who will believe their own shucks. When they are told that honesty is the best policy they believe it and so when they say it, they probably believe it too, even though they cheat on their income tax and recognize the value of the strategic or "little white" lie. I'm not necessarily making a moral judgment about believing in one set of values and saying you believe in another. I am mainly suggesting that this kind of separation produces fragmentation in the human psyche, of the sort which leads to a legion of protective and often destructive mechanisms that screw up the person and his society.

Now, as I have implied throughout, I am convinced that shucking exists at every level of social functioning, but my own specialty is school shucking, so that is what I am going to talk about. If this were to be one of my typical academic essays the Shuck title would be "The Organization of the Shuck in the Educational Context," but I won't use it. My purpose is only to help you see how people in schools go about shucking each other.

There have been many books, of late, which have it in for the schools, which seek methodically to expose the painful contradictions in American education. This is not that kind of book. Most of us sense what is wrong with the schools and do not need to be told that there are problems, or weaknesses. For better or worse that case has been made by men like Kohl and Kozol and Denison. Their criticisms focused on, among other things, the way in which schools wreck the lives of black kids in the ghetto. This was important to state, and now that most of us are well aware of the atrocities of ghetto education it is time to expand our consciousness and consider how we all get sucked into the game, regardless of sex, age, race or social-class background. There are many people in education who are working hard to make changes, to correct the inequities. Their success or failure does not depend upon yet another critique of public education.

What I want to do is to analyze and describe, in as light a vein as the subject will allow, the problems we have in everyday schooling and to suggest, as best I can what the possibilities are for reviving the educational system.

To do all this I need to draw upon my years as a public school teacher and college professor, my skill as a sociologist, and my talent as a creative writer. To only the first can I testify. For about ten years now I have been writing about schools and people involved in them. For the most part I have concentrated on the social aspects of schools and schooling. Unfortunately—and I haven't always known it was unfortunate—I have conducted these literary affairs in a schizophrenic manner. Like other American shuckers I have done one kind of writing because it was me and another kind because it paid off. This is my first attempt to consolidate the two.

I taught in the public schools for six years. I was a white teacher in an all black school, a white teacher in an all white school, and had short stints in about every other kind of school. I have taught elementary, secondary, and college, undergraduate and graduate. For the past nine years I have been a college professor observing how the baby shuckers and the juvenile shuckers and the adolescent shuckers have become mature shuckers. College, I believe, is the greatest shuck of them all. It brings the winners together for their final and most competitive stretch of shucking.

I return to the schools now and then to see what new versions of the old shucking games still predominate. I come away always amused at variations that never would have occurred to me; if they had I probably would have used them. I am almost never offended at the deceits anymore, but I am sometimes saddened that we have not provided students with an environment in which they can be themselves. I feel the same way when the shuck is directed specifically at me, as when a student has to convince me that he either needs to get into a closed class or get a B out of one that he was never really in.

In one sense, and I hesitate to say it, since I have already alerted you to the shucking game, this book could be viewed as one approach to the study of education. The careful reader will be suspicious at this point. The thought that should be crossing his or her mind is, "Aha, here he is trying to regain academic respectability."

Be that as it may, I am attempting to describe social processes at work within the school through the vehicle of the shuck game. In this sense the game is equivalent to the institutionalized patterns of interaction that we observe in schools. The way in which persons choose to act, in performance of their learned roles, tells us a great deal about the kind of game they are playing and the kind of park in which they play.

The book is not dry sociology, which may be redundant, even though some of the terms are sociological jargonese. The people are players in a socio-drama which is familiar to us all, but they are also real. You will encounter school administrators, teachers, students, parents, counselors in various shapes and sizes. Hopefully, the characters become more than the prototypes of sociology. They do not, however, again hopefully, become villains and innocents. Do not look for evil in the persons, for demonic bureaucrats plotting for personal gain. They may very well be there but they are not the villains. They are the victims even when they are the victors, for the cost of victory in the shucking wars is the surrender of the soul, the loss of integrity, the loss of the self that might have been.

Schools will always be social systems, containing norms, values, status symbols and the like. But this does not mean that shucking will always exist. It is theoretically possible to build social structures in which the base morality is honesty and a genuine concern for the growth and well being of others. In order to produce people who behave by these new norms we have to begin by considering whether or not the old structures have outlived their usefullness. By looking at these structures through the mechanism of the shucking game we can, perhaps, find part of an answer.

In the classroom, the shucking game as played by the teacher becomes a process of molding the personalities of children through a series of mysterious shapings such as:

"All right children, I want you all to think of a color. Good, that's right, close your eyes and think. All right Mary, now what color did you think of?"

"Green, teacher."

"I'm sorry Mary, that's wrong."

Now, let us go in search of the rule.

CHAPTER ONE

The Ritualism— Loyalty Shuck

"I pledge leisance to the flag of the United States of Merica and to the public which it stands on one nation invisible with liberty and justice for all."

"Class, be seated."

The fact that most students don't get it right until about the fifth grade tells us something about the way we instill loyalty and patriotism into our future citizens—through rituals.

Institutions have functions to perform. The school is supposed to take care of such functions as skill training, social mobility, and the development of qualities of good citizenship. Loyalty and patriotism are, inseparably, part of that responsibility.

When I was a teacher in a high school we had a paper drive. Schools have drives all the time—cookie drives, copper pipe drives, PTA drives. You know about drives. Well, the school wasn't doing too well and the principal was upset. His name was Frederich Trope. He had a way of never accepting the blame for anything himself, even if he was clearly at fault. He stood up on the stage in the auditorium and blasted everybody, teachers, counselors, students, and even the custodian for burning paper in the trash can instead of bringing it out to the sidewalk where the drive was being held. His speech went something like this:

"We will be the laughing stock of the city. We are about 50 tons of paper behind everybody. [He made up statistics.] Where is your spirit, your pride, your loyalty to Roger Cuney High School? Where is your loyalty to each other? Where is your loyalty to yourselves?" He never said "Where is your loyalty to me?" but everybody in the room knew that is what he meant. He was the only person who really cared about the damn drive at all.

As I said his name was Trope. I'll have occasion to refer to him again in other contexts. The important thing about school principals is that they personify the process by which values are adopted in schools and, ultimately, in society: that is, power and fear. Some interesting techniques also combine with force to constitute the substance of our life in school. One that is associated with loyalty is the technique of hero worship. The school that Mr. Trope ruled was named after an early nineteenth-century western naturalist and explorer whom we'll call Roger Cuney. Mr. Trope had a very positive regard for Roger Cuney, but I wonder if he would have felt the same way if the school wasn't named after him. Trope dug up an old portrait of Cuney somewhere and purchased, out of student body funds, a grand golden frame. The portrait was hung over his desk where Trope could carry on an ongoing conversation with the portrait, which he did frequently.

The interesting point, I think, is that no one in the school objected to the use of student body funds to purchase the frame because—the way it was presented—it would have appeared to be extreme disloyalty to contest it. We were, teachers and students alike, cast into a ritualistic worship of Roger Cuney. This occurred in numerous ways, from all-day assemblies dedicated to his memory (which usually included a dull talk by an old forest ranger who remembered seeing Cuney in the woods when the ranger was a small boy), to social studies lessons, to writing the name every time one wrote the school, to brief announcements that the principal would make over the loudspeaker whenever he or anyone else found a biographical item. The power of that force which turned us into Cuney worshipers is aptly demonstrated by the fact that the most significant thing Roger Cuney ever did was to spend a month in the mountains by himself and write a very uninteresting book about it.

Nonetheless Roger Cuney, like Washington, Jefferson, and Lincoln, became the model for all virtues, for all good, respectable behavior. We were trained to care, to imitate, and to be loyal to the name. So when we fell down in the paper drive we were told we were being disloyal to the memory of Roger Cuney. And some of us felt ashamed of ourselves, as if we had let the American flag fall to the ground during the "raising" ceremony.

Another technique for instilling loyalty is to get students to say something in a ritualistic way, like the lord's prayer or the pledge of allegiance. It is usually better to avoid discussion of words since talking about them somehow seems to rob them of the spiritual quality. Looking back, and some of us looking on, it surely seems somewhat absurd that we could get choked up during our school songs, but there were many forces making that possible. We always knew, for example, that all crimes against the school being equal, committing one during the flag raising, pledge of allegiance, bible reading, or singing the school song made it more serious. When I was a kid I used to have an almost uncontrollable urge to scream out "I hate Miss Stevens" (my fourth-grade teacher), during the singing of the school song, or during the pledge, and once or twice during the bible reading. I never felt the urge any other time. Later on, when I worked as a substitute teacher in some of the toughest city schools I sacrilegiously used the bible to protect my sanity. When students were beyond calling to order or anything else I would pick up the bible and start reading from it in a low voice. Eventually I had quiet. Sometimes I would read for hours.

Now back to Cuney High. Put them all together—Mr. Trope in his most reverent pose, on the stage with hands raised like a conductor to lead us in singing, students standing in rigid lines, the school banner waving proudly above us, teachers watching for the slightest disturbance, and the announcement, in respectful voice.

"And now, the school song, 'Dear Cuney High,' [Pause] ready, begin . . ."

I think there are millions of people in this country who, if you stood over their bed in the middle of the night and said softly, "ready begin," would stand up and either recite the pledge of allegiance, or sing their high school song.

DEAR HIGH, DEAR CUNEY HIGH
OUR STANDARDS WE RAISE ON HIGH

Some of the kids would really get into it, even some who, I remember, didn't have the slightest chance of graduating.

FORTUNE AND GLORY
FOREVER WILL BE THINE

This brings us to another strategy for instilling loyalty. That is, since reverence is such a decadent and generally un-American value, given the "equality of all men" principle, the way we can raise the value of men and things above those that are less equal is to use decadent and un-American language—like Thine.

LOYALTY AND HONOR
WILL BE OUR GRACIOUS SIGN

I would guess that most of us can differentiate between things that make sense and things that just feel right. Actually, I imagine the quality of feeling improves to the degree that the meaning escapes us.

WHEREVER FATE MAY LEAD ME
WHEREVER I MAY BE
MY HEART WILL SEND ME HOMEWARD
IN MEMORIES OF THEE

And so forth. I think the point has been made. It is interesting to speculate on why certain sentiments continue despite the fact that history has shown each of us personally that it never happens that way. How many of us have stood on a faraway shore and had memories of our own Roger Cuney High School? And if we did have memories were they about the glory and the honor or about the girl we made love to in the back seat of the car behind the gym, before, after, or during the prom or the game.

Now the central point of this chapter is not about school songs or colors, or devotions to our flag and country, or even to God. It is about the strategy that we employ in schools to bring about certain attitudes and behaviors. I am talking about *ritualism;* that is, learning through ritual.

I would argue, and of course have, that learning does not take place as a result of ritual, although what we say and how we act is produced by it. But, I think, this is the worst of us as human beings. I believe I was well into high school before I sensed that democracy and patriotism and America were distinctly different concepts. My teachers kept telling me that we lived in a democracy, we are a democracy, we believe in democracy, we believe in America. I was also led to believe that schools in democracies were democratic schools, so when I stood up for my school and my country I was standing up for democracy, against communism, against fascism.

My intention is not to suggest that we aren't a democracy; it's just that I never learned what one was, probably because it is hard to learn about democracy in a fascist school. I think this says something about the psychology of learning. Whatever things are, we do not come to truly understand them by being told what they are or that we are part of them. One learns about democracy by having a democratic experience. But in my school life I was told to do everything I ever did. And today it is still the same in most places.

In some schools ritualism and rigidly enforced loyalty do not structure the interaction between people. It might be instructive to think about what an alternative to the conventional model might look like. The alternative is a place where teachers do not con their kids into believing that the world is good and beautiful and that their country has no faults and their school no problems. These are schools where the problems of democracy and conventional structures like family, church, and economic opportunity are questioned. I am not just talking about ghetto or barrio schools where black and Chicano teachers know who they are and know the kids can tell a shuck as well as they can, although in my own experience this is the most likely place to find this kind of honesty in student-teacher relationships. Still, there are many classrooms where loyalty to a way of life called democracy, or American, or "our way" is questioned and discussed, and there are some teachers who take the risk that students are mature enough not to think of questioning as subversion. I think, perhaps, the earlier we teach kids to question, the less likely it is we'll get them in our college classes labeling us "pinko" because we ask if things are the way they should be.

Also, an alternative structure is one where the decision making is truly participatory democracy. This is harder to find than isolated nonritualistic teachers. But some school administrators are around who have gone through a series of student demand sessions and come out a little more sensitive to the desire of students to have some input in decisions. The students may not yet get to make the decisions, but their concerns are aired and often influence the process.

There will be more about alternative structures as we go along. In the final chapter I talk about a way of checking out alternatives, and I will attempt to relate the issues throughout the book to this model. But let's get back to some significant experiences, like the time I worked as a supervisor of student teachers.

I was sitting in the back of a third-grade class watching the teacher, an attractive young girl about 21 or 22 conduct a lesson in ways of American life during the era of the early settlers. She was a student teacher who had been in the classroom about 15 weeks with someone called a master teacher. This is where they learned how to be a teacher. I had spoken to the girl before class and I must begin the description with the most pollyanna of all comments; she meant well. This was no archaic spinster of educational legend whom most of us had at one time or another. She was a bright, recent college graduate, who loved kids and had the best of intentions.

She spent the first half hour of the lesson reading statements to the class and they were to be graded on how neatly they wrote them in their notebooks. The statements went as follows:

Number 1, Our forefathers, the early settlers, were courageous.

Number 2, Our forefathers brought liberty to our shores.

At this point a little boy raised his hand to ask about liberty and she answered in good pedagogic fashion, "Look it up in the dictionary after the lesson George, and then you'll know what it is."

Number 3, Our forefathers believed that all men were created equal.

On and on went the commendations and slogans that we could all repeat in our sleep. But nowhere was an attempt made to produce an understanding of "courageous," "liberty," or human "equality." And nowhere would such an attempt be made because educational institutions intend that we learn by definition, which we are given; by ritual, which we practice; and by examination, which we despise.

Again, the alternative is what? Questioning, participation, individualizing. Just getting away from ritualizing by allowing students to make up their own minds about how things are and to feel free to test their own ideas out on the teacher and others.

But let's turn now to the college campus where the final part of the formal learning process takes place. We might begin by talking about the "hallowed halls of ivy" to maintain the spirit of our current theme:

ritual, loyalty, and time-honored styles of making it all come out "right."

On the campus, despite our best attempts to be "relevant" and up to date, there remains a trace of history. It's not always obvious but some of the old traditions still remain, and they have an impact on the lives of persons who inhabit the campus. Again, it is important to note that traditions, slogans, rituals of whatever sort may not, in themselves be either good or bad. But the way that they structure our lives, and influence our learning may damage us, to the point where we neither live nor learn.

Let us begin with a living stereotype, the professor with the tweedy coat and pipe, dropping ashes all over his lecture notes. Often he is one of the younger members of the faculty. He hasn't quite caught on yet to the reality that universities are corporate bureaucracies. He still wanders around the libraries with several moldy manuscripts under his arm and he still forgets everything and notices nothing. If he is a younger member of the faculty he may want to do something important and meaningful, which means that he will not get promoted since it takes longer to do something like that than the department will allow you. Some students respect these professors even though they know that they are not quite with it.

What also remains of history are the remmants of the old elitist style of living and interacting. Ivy league schools still provide their scholars with the rich and pleasantly decadent surroundings for formal and informal gatherings. I remember a very pleasant luncheon in the faculty club at Columbia. I recall the large red leather chairs, the aged oaken tables, the grand windows and heavy curtains that reminded me of a box at the opera, and the delicately served food. And I remember in the middle of the meal I noticed below me the wide expanse of Harlem.

On most campuses, as on mine, faculties are divided up between tenured and untenured members. Even though this structure can be manipulated for such bureaucratic purposes as rewarding conformists and punishing radicals, there still remains some of the grand traditional design. Being a tenured faculty member myself, not having found any significance in my professional life prior to being promoted, I am invited to participate in the deliberations of this privileged faculty.

Those of us who have any social science background come to realize, as we look about us on these occasions, that we perpetuate what we study, an elitist, stratified society.

This little group, like other fraternities, has its traditions and conventions and, above all, its secrets. Or maybe, above all it has its responsibilities. Many prefer to think of it that way. At a recent meeting one of my "esteemed colleagues" (they talk like that at these meetings) rose to comment that it was our responsibility to look after the welfare of the untenured faculty. It was said much in the manner of a lord talking about the welfare of his serfs. At any rate, we feel we have our responsibilities as well as our secrets. The secrets are functional, of course. If we are going to look out for the welfare of the younger faculty we want to be absolutely certain that they don't know about it, or they might misunderstand. They might misunderstand the fact that when we fire them it is for their own welfare. It takes time to groom people to understand the burdens of responsibility, or as it might have been put in the old days, the burdens of the crown.

The alternative that is suggested in this instance is an open evaluation process, where those without status or longevity are at least permitted input and the right to face their evaluators. To be really radical the alternative would be to permit other nontenured faculty and/or student representation on evaluating committees. Many colleges and universities have moved in this direction but it is still a long time away until the traditional status structures atrophy.

The first lecture I ever gave as a university professor showed that I had learned the rituals well. After a number of years as a high school and junior high school teacher I was personally inclined to be somewhat informal but I had the distinct impression that my college students expected something with a little more professional style. So I kept my jacket on and stood rigid in front of the lectern and had my notes neatly typed out and used as many big words as I could think of and made references to esoteric books that I had never read. I did the same kind of thing for several years. Then I figured that this traditional image idea was my own hangup, so I decided to give my students the benefit of the real me.

I walked into my first class of the year, took my jacket off, sat on the desk, and said "Hi, I'm Carl Weinberg."

This was followed by bedazzled silence.

"OK," I said, "enough of this bureaucratic bullshit, let's start talking to each other." ("Bullshit" was to become the most common term on campus a few years later.)

There was buzzing and some nervous giggles and people looking at each other.

"I don't have a reading list for this course because I don't yet know what you're going to be interested in," I said, "and I won't give you my office hours because we can get together any time we're both free. Any questions?"

After a few eternal seconds somebody in the front row raised a tenative hand, "Excuse me Dr. Weinberg."

"Call me Carl," I said without making a fuss.

"Yes, Dr. Weinberg, I wanted to know about tests and term papers."

"Please call me Carl, "I repeated. "What about them?"

"How many will there be?" she asked sheepishly.

I looked over the class and I could see that they weren't getting the point.

"I'm not sure," I said. "We'll have to decide that together."

There followed another long silence. There was a great deal of tension in the room. I'm not sure how one knows these things. There can be other reasons for silence. I was feeling pretty good as I remember. It was the start of a new life style and I could sense that. But I was having some trouble getting the students to fall in line.

It took about an hour for the class to relax behind my informality and just before the session ended I asked for final questions on my general orientation. One student in the back raised his hand and after being assured that he could feel free to speak up without the old hand-raising convention he nodded uncomfortably and said, "Dr. Weinberg, are you going to grade on the curve?"

My personal failure was made certain, of course, by the fact that I was meeting with the students in a formal setting. I just bet if my first class was held in a tavern I might have broken through. The alternative structure that I am hinting at would have to be one where the setting for interaction was deformalized. I think this is coming. Faculty are giving up their uniforms gradually, more classrooms are being arranged in circles, fewer rituals with required formal attendance are being held. We're a few years away, but we're getting there.

One way of recognizing a ritual and distinguishing it from a functional act is to think about meaning. That is, why some things are done. Why, for example, do we grade on the curve? Why do we grade at all? Why do we assign books, why do we read them? Why does the professor or teacher command the action rather than the student?

"Things just aren't done that way; it's a matter of professionalism." This was the response I got from one of my deans when I let it be known that I intended to have my students evaluate themselves. One of our untenured faculty was taken apart by the higher-ups when he proposed the same method of evaluation in a class of over 700.

When you ask the average student why he is graded, he can't tell you. When you ask the average dean or chancellor or college president he can't really tell you either although his shuck demands that he give it a try. The point at issue is beyond debate because it is part of the ritual of college education. Since, except in technical specializations, most of college life exists as it does only because it has always been that way, when one attacks the conventions he, in fact, attacks practically everything college *is*. It's time that we admitted to being a ritual, part of the sociological rite of passage from one status to another.

There are certain nasty realities which we have to face in supporting the existence of colleges if we admit that they have little functional value. First, there is the problem of what to do with the young people if they didn't go to college. Second, there is the issue of helping industrial magnates sort out the liver from the filet mignon. Third, there is the matter of finding a place for intellectuals and scientists to work.

Very few people have any doubt that we can grind out persons in all occupational categories without 90 percent of the courses students take but, since we have to detain them to keep the work force fluid we might as well give them Chaucer and nineteenth-century Paraguayan history and the economics of Afghanistan between the two world wars. This is not to say that I am against ideas or intellectual pursuits; I am only against the tradition of requiring students to take hundreds of units, for a grade, to get them into the job market.

The college student himself is obsessed with ritual. He has been trained to concern himself specifically with the manner of survival. Since when does understanding come into it? "I have to take classes, mid-terms and finals; write term papers, with footnotes arranged in certain ways; sit in class and take notes; register for classes; wait in long lines for physicals, classes, checks, food, books; buy books, read select parts, sell back books, buy new ones; check out books for term papers; study; and try to get a date for the weekend.''

There are ritualistic ways of getting through college, ways of talking professors out of work, and counselors out of requirements, while acting as if one is a true believer. A girl who just left my office told me that she heard how exciting my class was and how real learning was going on and how it was relevant. Oh yes, and could she get credit for the course even if she didn't have time to come to the classes since she was working on a significant social reform project?

The alternative to the grade-seeking, career allocation ritual is to somehow separate colleges and universities from the business of certifying for careers. Give that over to industry and let them train and sort out the people they want or need. They could probably do it better anyhow. This plan too is on the drawing board at one of our larger think factories and may be coming. I'm sure I wouldn't approve of the way industry would go about sorting out, but in this book that's not my business. If we can free the university from its loyalty to the job market, we'll have made a good start toward playing the learning game again.

The ritualism-loyalty shuck involves a number of considerations. Like most shucks, this one is reciprocal, but not as reciprocal as many others. By this I mean that shucks are usually beneficial to all participants in them, but in somewhat different ways.

For example, although teachers and principals demand a certain kind of ritualistic loyalty from the kids, the kids can shuck the hell out of them by appealing to this loyalty. Suppose a student comes in late. He faces three detentions. Unless he says something like:

> "I would have been here on time Mr. Fishman but I had to stop over my aunt's house to pick up some papers for the paper drive so our homeroom could win."
> "So where are the papers?"
> "She didn't have any."

Ordinarily, however, teachers and administrators use the shuck of loyalty to the school, or class, or flag, or country as a source of last appeal to which they can always apply some standard for getting a kid to cooperate. I think the loyalty ritual is a way of organizing values around which schools can demand order, and usually conformity. It is an efficient way to have students put forth a greater effort to accomplish some standard routines, which is what school is all about. Oriental students are familiar with the notion of succeeding in order to maintain the integrity of the family name. This is a variation on that theme. Since most educators have few intrinsic motivators going for them in the classroom they need all the extrinsic ones they can get. Loyalty and ritual of the type we are representing are simply ways of maintaining a standard of performance which keep the morale, and consequently the routine order of school life, from falling apart. If we can't refer to the good old standards of Cuney High, where might students go for replacements? They might go to Bob Dylan or the Beatles or some other nontraditional source. And if there is one thing that schools must avoid it is an alternative set of standards.

It is hard to conceive of an educational institution without a "tradition" or unique configuration of standards of some sort. Sometimes these standards or conventions are highly individual, like the day we celebrate the namesake's birthday by stopping all routine studies and reading about his life in the great north woods. But usually the conventions can be generalized to most "old" schools. By "old" I simply mean not "new" schools. New schools seem to think they can get by without tradition or convention, but we all know that this will force them to rely exclusively upon interesting the student. The "old" school traditions are such things as saluting the flag, celebrating the birthdays of American "heroes," having an alma mater and singing it often, and competing for "our namesake" and the glory of our school with other schools. We also used to have a convention of reading the bible first thing in the morning and children always regarded this as sacred.

The loyalty shuck is often combined with the competition shuck to force kids to get themselves together in the school's way. When we compete with other schools or classrooms on assorted events we keep each other in line working for dear old victory. And, in this way, the teacher has an easier time of it.

I suppose to me the most obnoxious aspect of this particular shuck is the way we use these conventions to inspire the kids who are most abused by the system to support that system. We don't tell black kids that Washington was an elitist slaveholder but we get them to say "right on" when we tell them what a great man he was. They may not believe it but they know they better act as though they do. The same thing applies to our religious traditions and the bible. There has been nothing that has so held the black man back from demanding his liberation and equal opportunities in this life than the old Christian ethic, but that starts to run us into the morality shuck which bears a resemblance to it. We will talk about that later.

Now, how does focusing upon the rituals of educational life help us to see the possibilities for reconstructing education? What is the intent of the criticism of such enduring values as loyalty, patriotism, and tradition?

Perhaps I can come to it this way. When I was a boy I participated—and this word "participated" is important—in just about every esteemed American institution (church, family, school, country) without ever realizing that I had any choice. By the time I had reached high school I had squirmed out of religion, was half in and half out of school, was neutral about country, and was trying to make sense of the demands my family made upon me. As an adult and after years of struggle, I pretty much know where I stand in all areas. It is possible for me to live with all of them now, but it took a lot of understanding of the loyalty and conventions I was forced into as a youth. I guess I am saying that loyalty, in order to be an enduring quality of relationships, must be earned, not demanded. In this way, when formal attachments to the schools, families, or neighborhoods end, some emotional ties can still be constructively maintained. The same is true of ritual. There are some rituals I now enjoy very much, because I see how they are related to important human considerations, like the solidarity of groups or symbolic aesthetic experiences. Tim Leary, as antiestablishment as he was, adopted for his communal society a number of ritualistic kinds of behavior, taken from American Indian and Far Eastern rituals. Many of those who have rebelled against bureaucratic rituals are heavily into religious or cultural ones, particularly those taken from Eastern philosophy and religion.

So it is not ritual per se we must inspect but the ways it is used and the reasons we so use it. The point is that we now use ritual, symbolic loyalties, and attachments to grind out students in a kind of mechanical mold, so that they become the kind of students we can manage with minimum effort and the kind of citizens we can manipulate by appealing to their loyalty and training.

There is no doubt these strategies accomplish what they intend. But are these the outcomes we seek? Do we want robots as students and citizens, or do we want thinking, sensing, independent decision makers? My students reel and stumble in the face of freedom, in the face of the requirement to make their own decisions about what they want to do and how they want to do it. They would much rather be wound up and left to spin until they run down, and then restarted as when we do the "Ready Begin . . . I pledge a leisance . . .

To make it all come out differently we need to find a way to permit students to participate in their own education. We need to focus on the concept of choice, to consider at all times the ways in which we restrict choices or ritualize them. We need to *earn* loyalty rather than demand it, and the simplest way to do this is to help students see that they can use us as resources into exciting realms of learning. It is, again, unquestionably easier to mobilize and locomote vast numbers of students through the use of ritual and rule, than to use participation and freedom. We are an efficient society and the educational model is a duplicate of the one that mobilizes all of us in a mass industrial complex. When I think of this I always picture a ghastly cartoon with billions of tiny souls being efficiently transported across massive conveyor belts, stuffed with precision into cans, boxed by mechanical arms, and dropped into trucks with no drivers. On the sides of the conveyor belts, packages, boxes, and trucks are flags, Gods, presidents, and ghosts of our past, raising a finger to remind us, lest we forget, that we are part of a grand and glorious tradition.

So we have examined the ritual-loyalty shuck, which exists in the way that people want us to go along with offenses to our humanity in the name of convention, tradition, or "the rules." We are trained to believe in the way we are because it is the way we were and for no better reason than that. But we need a better reason. It might all come out the same, and we might do things the same way our fathers and forefathers did them, and we might end up believing in our God, our country, and our rules the way they did. But if we do, then we will know why, and that makes all the difference between ritualistic and meaningful living.

CHAPTER TWO

The Helping Shuck

One thing all children know is that adults are there to help them. They hear it all the time. "I am here to help you," "I want to help you," "I am doing it for your own good."

Children can take only so much help of the kind that most school personnel have to offer. "If you are here to help me," a child might ask, "why must I do everything your way?"

The helping shuck in schools consists of helping students achieve goals that they *should* have, even if they don't. The assumptions of this shuck are:

We know better, or best.

Someday you will understand and thank us.

You would want what we want you to want if you had our wisdom.

Our way is best because it is right, true, moral, godly, American and nice.

So students struggle under our dedicated service to them to become what we know is right for them to be. Their achievement in these areas is all the thanks we require for our sacrifice.

The educator's commitment to serve the needs of students is seldom questioned by the individual helper. Therefore, when a student fails, the burden of cause must fall on him alone. If we are certain we help students, then their failure must be seen as a failure to use our help. This kind of thinking extends the shuck to its limits, protecting the shucker against any possibility of failure himself. Has any one of you ever heard a teacher accepting the blame for any student's low grade?

When I was at Cuney High School I had a favorite student—whose name was George. George was a favorite because he was bright and an underdog and I had two stereotypes going for me right there. George was helped a lot around Cuney High. He was helped so much he became a dropout in spite of considerable intelligence.

I first noticed George in my English class. Schools, as we know, separate kids according to scores on tests. These tests contain some problems and drawbacks, but do the important job of giving us a basis on which to separate the nice kids from the not nice ones. This categorization is defended in helping terms. The intention is to help the nice kids by not holding them back, and the not nice kids by giving them more time for individual help, and thus keeping them from having a low self-image.

George was in, what we teachers called, the dumbbell class. This particular class was made up chiefly of vocational majors with a few female commercial students to give the class a sex balance. The females were selected by the counselors on the grounds that they wouldn't be offended when the male students said "mother fucker." There was little expectation that "that type" of female would graduate anyhow, so we weren't really standing in her way.

The thing I noticed about George was that he didn't seem to belong. He was, first of all, white. Almost all the other students in the class were black. Only George and one other boy, Tom Dealy, were white.

George seemed to be somewhat curious about what I had to say. He would even ask a question or two. Our first long chat took place after the first day of class. I asked him if there might not be a mistake about his being in the vocational curriculum and in this particular class. I'll never forget our conversation because it tuned me into much of the high school shuck game that I hadn't thought about before.

"I thought so too," he said, "but I guess it's right because Mr. Gallo, the counselor, told me that was how the tests came out."

I asked about those tests.

"I took a bunch of them," he told me, "and Mr. Gallo gave them to me himself because he is taking a course in testing."

I asked about the kind of tests.

"You know the ones, where they ask you if you want to spend your time in a shop full of machines or out in the woods with animals and stuff. I came out liking being around people and working with them but they sent me to the shop anyhow. It was because of the pattern."

"The pattern" is a good shuck term. Teachers and counselors and even parents look for patterns when they can't find evidence in some of the simple facts before them to support their prejudices. George told me how the pattern pointed toward him trying the vocational curriculum since he did so poorly in all the others. Later on I discovered that the data which made up this pattern were:

1. He couldn't spell
2. He turned in messy papers
3. He was frequently absent or tardy
4. His parents were separated and he didn't know his father's where-abouts
5. He was poor

So they put him in the shop even though his previous grades there were worse than in English and social studies, where neatness and spelling are important. The counselor, through a set of predetermined judgments, helped George into the industrial curriculum where he didn't want to be. He then helped Tom Dealy, the other white kid in my class, out of the industrial curriculum, even though he wanted to stay there.

George was a bright kid, not good looking enough to call forth the personal treatment that attractive students get, and not athletic enough to draw any attention from the coaches. Nonetheless he earned the structured help of the school because he was lucky enough to be a student. He received the routine processing all students get, regardless of anything. In my many chats with him over the next year and a half it became clear that George was the most pathetic sort of educational victim, one who knows what is happening to him, and is powerless to do anything about it.

Very few students fall into this category. Most students follow the sociological patterns established for them by society. Successful kids love success and get it and unsuccessful kids hate school for showing them up to be failures and turn off to it. And then there are the Georges of the world who intrinsically know that education has something worthwhile to offer them, but can't get into a position to demand it.

Tom Dealy, the other white boy in the class, who did belong, was an opposite kind of horror story. He had a driving passion for machines and tools and was one of the happiest industrial arts students I had ever seen, until they told him that he would have to leave because he was too intelligent to waste his time in the shop. His mother and his father and Mr. Gallo the counselor went at him like cops in the movies go after a confession. Within a week Tom consented to try the college prep course. Even after he flunked all his courses the first semester they wouldn't let him go back to the shop. He was declared an underachiever and left to underachieve the rest of his days. He dropped out about the same time that George did. I'll have more to say about both of them in other contexts.

The alternative that we need to seek in this regard is one that sees helping students as unrelated to sorting them homogeneously. The answer is obvious: separate them heterogeneously and find a way to solve the problems that this creates. Teachers and administrators will claim that this sort of grouping is inefficient since many different activities will have to be managed simultaneously. This is time consuming, hard on the teacher and expensive if—as is certain—additional resources are required. The response to this objection would have to be one that acknowledges the inefficiency, unless of course we train teachers to work this way rather than the way they typically work, teaching everybody simultaneously, as if they were all the same. Teachers would have to know how to organize small learning groups, set up learning centers for self-motivated individuals, and utilize available resources, such as other kids or parents or volunteers from the community. This is happening in many places. When I talk of alternatives I am not talking about ideal abstract proposals. I've seen these organizations work, and they solve the problems created by the helping shuck. It automatically eliminates the pretense of teachers that they are helping kids, when actually the efficiency requirements of the school force them to manipulate students in the manner most convenient to control and manage them.

Now I want to tell about my first trip to see a high school counselor, that helper among helpers. Her name was Mrs. Del Gado. I went to see her about a student of mine who I thought was a bit messed up in a very passive way. Mrs. Del Gado was Mr. Gallo's assistant and, I thought, vastly superior to him intellectually. Looking back it is evident that the reason he was head and she was assistant is because he was a *he* and she was a *she*, but that's another shuck in schools.

During the initial amenities, Mrs. Del Gado assured me that her job was to help teachers relate to students as much as it was to help students directly. I then discussed the student I was concerned about, starting by saying that he didn't cause me any trouble at all. He wasn't that kind of problem. I mean he wasn't the distracting student, the kind that most school "problems" seem to be.

"There are these compositions he writes." "They're strange."

"Strange?" she repeated.

"Morbid, I guess would be the word. His last composition was on spring, you know the usual about birds on the wing, flowers opening their buds and that sort, and within each trite paragraph he inserts odd things." (I read from the composition itself; I kept it for many years afterward.)

Spring is a lovely time of the year, flowers were blooming everywhere, everywhere but where I planted them. For me the flowers would never grow. In the spring I liked to catch worms and collect them together and then drop them in a can of boiling fat. The grass is green and the trees are too, I would catch snails on the leaves and we'd cut them up and pour salt on them to see them wiggle. Spring is a beautiful time of the year.

I stopped, thinking the point was obvious.

"Sadistic little devil, isn't he," Del Gado said.

"You say he never gives you any trouble in class?" she asked.

"None at all."

"There was one composition he wrote about chairs—fancy chairs, soft chairs, and then electric chairs, barber chairs, one in particular where a barber he read about would turn the chairs upside down and slit the customer's throat."

"You really think that there's something wrong with him?" Del Gado asked. "I mean rather than just unnatural morbidity?"

"I think so but how can you really know about those things. I just thought it might be important to call it to somebody's attention. I didn't feel I could just keep it to myself.''

"I can understand how you would feel that way," she said. Good counseling technique. I was concerned about the fact that I didn't seem to be connecting with her at all, even though she appeared to be attentive. As I said, I thought I was being obvious, but I knew nothing about the woman that I faced, except that she was about 45, married, and hoping for an appointment as a girls' vice principal in a school in a better neighborhood. Of all the gossip that circulated around our school, the most interesting was news of who was getting out, moving across town.

"Well I've just been wondering somewhat about facilities within the school system and I thought . . .''

"What kind of facilities do you have in mind?'' she asked, as if she had no idea what I was talking about.

I wanted to be careful not to imply any inadequacy to her or counselors in general, "just generally, the facilities for working within the home with some of the children whom we know to have psychological problems.''

She leaned back and gave it a moment's thought. "Do you have anything specifically in mind?''

"No," I told her, "but I was wondering, as I'm sure you have, if something more couldn't be done to help straighten out some of these kids, like this boy I'm talking about.''

She nodded, as if she wanted to be sure to acknowledge the fact that she had given it some thought and said, "Do you mean something on the order of a welfare worker?' '

"I suppose that would be close to what I mean," I conceded, hoping that would encourage her to go on.

"Well of course there's the child welfare and attendance worker.''

Could it be, I wondered, that she has forgotten about the boy and the bugs and the salt?

"Can we get somebody to talk to this boy I was telling you about?'' I asked.

She sat back in her chair then as if it was the first time that she understood what I was really trying to say.

"Well, I suppose I could talk to him for a bit, and find out if he was having troubles in school, but I thought you said that he wasn't that kind of problem.''

"No, he isn't. I mean he does OK in his grades."

"Yes," she said, "then I really don't see any purpose talking with him about problems that might have a good deal to do with his family or something on that order."

I didn't know what to say. I guess I must have shown disappointment.

"The boy may very well need some kind of help, Mr. Weinberg, but it appears that the kind of help he needs has nothing to do with the function of the school."

"But Mrs. Del Gado, some of these kinds of problems get in the way of kids learning well."

"But this hasn't happened yet with your boy, has it?"

"No, but . . ."

She went right on, "You're asking quite a bit of the school if you want us to be therapists," she said. "If we go that far we might as well try to rehabilitate the families and get the father a job and so on."

I stood up at that point. "I guess I haven't figured it all out, maybe I just don't know how things work."

"You'll learn," she said, "you appear to have a good head on your shoulders."

I thanked her and began to back out the door.

"Come in anytime," she said with a wave of the pencil, "if there's anything we can do to lend you a hand."

Counselors in this country have not changed a good deal over the past 20 years despite the explosion of therapeutic techniques and notions about the creation of therapeutic environments for learning. There is good reason for this static condition. It all rests on the conception of the word "help." What is really meant by "help" and who is it that is being helped?

Counselors, like teachers and administrators, owe their chief allegiance to the public, to the society, which employs them and maintains them in their position. Their function is to help society maintain its values in equilibrium, its economic structures in balance, and its statuses in upward motion.

To help a student against the best interests of society in general becomes for all educational personnel a contradiction of interests. Suppose a student came to a teacher and asked to be taught how to subvert the society. The request could come in any number of areas: He or she might want to blow up property to force the establishment to come around on some issue. He or she might want to start a free love commune looking toward alternative family patterns. The student might want to start an underground newspaper, make pornographic films, or paint abstractions eight hours a day. Can a teacher help him to do these things? How about something really hard, like helping a kid go through school without taking tests or being graded or put into a track curriculum? Can we help him?

An alternative conception of counseling is one that shifts the function away from the rehabilitation of "problem" children, whose only problems may be that they annoy teachers, to the reorganization of the environment such that it is therapeutic for all students and others who inhabit the school. The counselor would be responsible for advising administrators about the structures that hurt the individual, or the group, and those which help. The shuck is avoided in this new arrangement because the latent focus can no longer be controlling or managing students in the name of helping them since, by definition, the counselor would be more interested in change than in stability. I realize this latter conception of helping leaves some kids who have problems without a place to go to deal with them, but for the most part this kind of help is seldom available anyhow, and if our new kind of counselor is doing the job we talked about, fewer problems will emerge in the first place. A therapeutic environment should be seen as one that does not create the problems in the first place. The process of creating healthy environments requires a grasp of the structures that are not healthy, and these are outlined in Chapter Ten for anyone who might be able to use the system approach to producing healthy children, as well as adults.

The process of helping kids by sorting them out from each other and keeping them away from each other has got to be one of the most invidiously cruel shucks of public education. A friend of mine teaches a group referred to in my state as EH, or educationally handicapped. This is in a public school in a middle-class neighborhood. His stories about his life among the stigmatized, when he is not being humorous, are portraits of mystification. The dishonesty begins in the account of the efforts educators undertake in order to give these unfortunates very special treatment. They have the best teacher-pupil ratio in public education. They have good equipment and materials. They have special buildings. They have visiting psychiatrists, psychologists, dance therapists, and art therapists, all of whom are conducting experiments on the pupils. And with it all they are treated like a bunch of monkeys in a cage surrounded by the sanity of middle-class education. As my friend likes to put it, "just picture a walled insane asylum in the middle of Harvard University."

"To top it off," he tells me, "not only don't the school administrators allow any contact between our kids and their kids, the regular teachers treat me and the other EH teachers like the kids treat the kids. They won't even let us eat with the rest of the faculty."

Part of the shuck, as I understand it, comes from how they use these kids. My friend tells me that they have at least ten visiting dignitaries a week, and that's not counting the researchers. "They won't let us eat with them," he says, "but we can perform for them all we want." I checked this out myself and he's right. It is a big act, with everybody performing for everybody else: the principal putting on a show for the visitor from New Guinea, and the teacher putting on a show for the principal, and the kids putting everybody on. They really aren't that sick but they know that visitors expect them to act strange so they do. Then, when the visitors leave, the kids laugh, feeling like the big put-on redeems them just a bit for all the indignities that they are made to suffer, in the name of receiving special help.

The solution to the problem of retarded children is not possible in an educational structure that assumes differentiation and allocation as its prime function. Some solution to the problem of inhumane treatment of some kids—the confused, the poor, the handicapped, the minorities—is only possible in an environment which permits children the freedom to define themselves in human terms rather than forcing definitions on them in educational terms. We need to do away with failure in conventional terms—that is, setting kids against each other so some of them lose out. But more than this we need to eliminate the categories of implicit failure, the categories that all kids, from about the third grade up, understand. I am talking about such cracks as "educationally handicapped," "social adjustment," "industrial," "vocational," or "commercial," "upward bound," "culturally disadvantaged," "enrichment programs," "fifth quintile," and the like.

These categories are often made to sound respectable but they really make the shuck just a little bit more obvious. Not long ago a representative of the executive branch of the state government, a retired army general, approached me and a colleague at the university to suggest a program of educational help for ghetto kids entitled "Save the Children." The intention was to take a group of black and Chicano kids out of their community and put them away for a period of time in a deserted army camp where we could give them fun and education and a message that would help them see the value of getting themselves and their parents off the welfare roles. I refused to cooperate with the general-turned-educator, but I'm sure that his program, or programs under similar names with similar intentions are being supported at the highest political levels. The point is, if one has a good title and a good name for the program, you can pull off almost any shuck. But everybody knows that.

At the university we had a program entitled "High Potential." How's that for dealing with the stigma which never quite wore off? Its new title is so complicated that I only remember the initials, which I suppose was the intent. The program offered a helping hand to black, brown (Chicano) and some red and yellow students in the form of scholarships. In addition to the money, we help by lowering our admissions criteria. Many of my colleagues also help by pushing the grades up for these students, to keep them in school.

Despite this significant effort, a good portion of these students drop out or flunk out. Many of them just get bored. I had a conversation with one of my minority fellowship students the other day. It went something like this:

I started, "Lou, I don't mind you showing up an hour late for class but at least try to find out what we're talking about before you start to argue with me."

"Ah, you professors are all alike. You just like to sit up there and bullshit and the stuff you talk about is completely irrelevant."

"That might be," I granted, "but I don't know how you would know since you come only every sixth time and even then it's an hour late for a two-hour class."

"Ah come on professor, you know I have to have two jobs besides coming here. We're not like your average WASP student who gets his check from his daddy on the first of the month."

I granted that too. "But you're not going to get the grades to keep up your scholarship," I warned him. "It's one thing to get you in but it's another to keep you in."

"Don't give me that bullshit," he said, "we couldn't stay in anyhow."

"What do you mean" I asked? I think I already knew but I wanted his perspective.

"I mean that we can't understand those lectures and those tests. They don't mean anything to me."

"You could get tutorial help," I said.

"No, I can't," he said.

I figured he was right. "Have you tried?"

"Sure I tried."

"Where did you try?"

"I didn't know where to try."

"So what did you do," I asked him.

"Took another job."

I've been trying for a couple of years to get some programs going to which minority students can relate, but it's hard. Most of my colleagues think that helping stops when you let people get in. To me that's like helping somebody over the fence into a yard that's ruled by two hungry Doberman pinschers.

The "high potential" students get slaughtered. They look around for what they call "survival" courses. Those are courses where professors will give a C just for showing up, sometime.

I taught a course that I thought would help black students and white students alike a couple of years back called "Education in Black and White." Students sat around and talked to each other about their different perspectives on their educational experiences. In the course were all the "black course regulars," black students who took any course having anything to do with race relations. They figured it was one subject they knew something about without reading all the books. By the third time the course was offered we had over 500 students trying to get in, and we took about 200. The consequences were disastrous. Many of the students had important growth experiences. They learned about themselves and how their ethnic history was different from others. They also did a lot of reading. For them it was an important course. Unfortunately, many of the students treated the course as an easy shuck on the one hand and a sexual opportunity on the other. These students ruined it for the legions who might have come after. The professionals in my department killed the course by cutting it back to a minimum number of students, I think about 30, and refusing to permit anyone but myself to teach it. Since I was going on a sabbatical, the course died, and I was the only one who seemed to care. The liberals on the committee who killed the program advised me that we don't help anyone by lowering standards. They were all for helping but they wanted to find a professional way to do it. That was several years ago and we still haven't found a way.

The alternative to helping students in and washing them out has got to be one that reverses the second phase, the washout. It is a program that has an extensive orientation dealing with how to survive in college, the kinds of skills ghetto kids don't typically pick up on the streets. Some colleges try this and it works for some students, but it is tough to make up for eighteen years of academic survival socialization (a natural process if you are white and middle class) in one quarter or semester. This kind of a program needs a tutorial system working with it, but even this won't be sufficient help for the majority. The only answer for the large number of high-potential type students, who have ability but not the form that most professors require is to open the class up to different ways of getting grades. Rapping for example, could replace writing a term paper. Another way to help is to relate the content of the course to the students' own background and then go on from there. But again, helping students is usually a mattter of helping them meet everybody's goals but their own and doing it everybody's way but their own. The point is, if the opportunity programs are not in themselves to be a shuck, we must make realistic efforts to help the student succeed.

I really never have completely figured out how to help students in general. My classes are usually closed out after the first day but I have a reputation for helping out minority students, so they come around about the third week of the course and want to get in. If I turn them down I'm a liberal fascist. If I let them in I'm a sucker. In the past I used to let in as many blacks and browns as came around, because I teach a sociology course and race is big in sociology these days. Besides, I like lively discussions and the black students contribute heavily to these, mainly by calling all the white students "mother fucking racists." That was OK; we could work our way out of that. But when I got hung up in the problem of getting the black students to attend the discussions so they could make their unique contribution, that seemed to them a lot to ask.

After I threatened them with examinations and the like they started coming to class, about a half hour to an hour late. When I complained about that they called me a bourgeois bureaucrat who was all hung up in middle-class affectations like punctuality. We discussed that too but it was obvious that the issue isn't a rational one.

No matter what I do to help students, it doesn't work out the way I thought it would. When I stopped giving examinations on the books, students stopped reading the books. When I stopped giving exams on lectures they stopped coming to class. When I stopped lecturing and started leading discussions they didn't know how to discuss anything. They wanted me to go back to lecturing and when I did that, again they told me I was "irrelevant."

Last summer I decided to try to help students find some relevance in their education because we had just had a strike and a minor riot in the spring and the time seemed right for a little innovation. We started by meeting on the lawn, which they liked. I gave them a list of about six books I thought they might like to read, which were pertinent to the course, "The Sociology of Education." Then I told them about the contract system I had worked out to handle the grade problem. They could get so many points for this and so many for that and end up with a grade. At first, they liked that idea too.

They wore out my contract system bit by bit. First they went to work on the reading points. I had offered them five points for every book on the list that they read, but I wanted a brief report. They wanted me to trust them on the book reports but I said I needed to have some evidence, so they shifted their strategy. They suggested that instead of my choosing the books, they should have the right to choose the books in line with their own interests and needs. I couldn't argue with that so I agreed. The book reports started coming in and I knew I had lost the first round. One of the white students read *Run Dick Run* and said it was relevant because it showed that public school reading was biased to the middle class. I had to grant that. About eight of the black students turned in a report on the *Autobiography of Malcolm X* which would have been fine except I knew that they had all read it in the past. Some of them had turned the same report in to me a year before. So I asked them to do another one. The white students had their own variation of *Malcom X*, Salinger's *Catcher in the Rye*, which they were all required to read in freshman English.

I offered them 50 points for an ethnography. I figured this would certainly be relevant to the kinds of experiences they always complained about not having. They had to choose some ethnic group and go out and find data and have interviews and take pictures and read books and turn in a project showing what it meant to be white or black or Oriental or Jewish in the schools. There were dozens of other topics too, like radicals and hippies and school administrators. I was really looking forward to these projects but I didn't get many of them. The problem was that, having organized the little project groups so that they were ethnically heterogeneous, they couldn't agree about a topic. Some groups took the entire quarter to decide on a topic and when they decided, it was too late to do anything about it so they wrote a report on relating to each other. I couldn't turn this down but I only gave partial credit. Some groups broke down because the black students refused to work with the white ones. That caused me a lot of trouble.

Then there were their individual projects for which I offered 30 points. Most students did something in this area but it was probably something that they either did in the past or had to do anyhow. One guy went to army reserve camp for a week and wrote a report on that. A girl went to her friend's Jewish wedding and did a paper on a cross-cultural experience.

I don't help students much any more. I really don't know how. Or if I do help them, I don't think of it as helping. One of my students came in the other day and told me that she had broken her engagement to a medical student, quit her job, and had been rejected by her parents; all because I helped her find relevance in her academic life. I don't want the responsibility any more.

I suppose, in the throes of my current disappointment, I am suggesting that helping students means helping them to survive, not to learn. By relaxing the requirements in my course, hoping to encourage self-motivation, I really helped them do better in the other courses they were taking. By talking about "relevant" issues, in their terms I am helping them to relieve the boredom of the long haul through college.

If it wasn't clear at the beginning, I want to make the point now that, in every sense, the shuck game runs two ways. Students learn to give as much as they get. "After all," one of my undergraduates told me the other day, "you don't play football on a tennis court. What you give is what you get."

The heart of the helping shuck is that it is hard to find a point where helping involves bending—really bending. Rather than change a strategy, theory, assignment, technique, or whatever in order to help a person, we develop an elaborate rationale to label what we do anyhow as helping. This is called mystification. It is a giant shuck because it not only involves us in something we shouldn't be doing, it also requires that we justify it on some moral grounds. I suppose the best example of this is our country's involvement in Vietnam. It is one thing to kill a large number of our young men and the young and old men, women, and children of southeast Asia to maintain economic and political influence there; it is another to say that we are doing it to make the world safe for democracy, to help our yellow brothers and sisters throw off the yoke of totalitarianism. We have all heard the My Lai rationale, that we had to destroy the village in order to save it. Well, education has its own brand of mystification in this area. We destroy boys and girls in order to help them.

Another way of saying the same thing is that there is *really* helping and there is *institutionalized* helping. We assume that because we give a kid 12 years of free education we are helping him do something he wants to do. Another way of looking at the same experience is that we require kids to stay in school until they are 16 or so in order to make them into something that we need them to be. Really helping involves giving something more than we are routinely hired to give. It requires this notion of bending, which I mentioned before. Bending means putting forth a bit more effort than is necessary to keep our jobs.

Educators like to think of themselves as people who help, who give. They are men and women in service to society. The big shuck starts right there. For every educator I have known to be truly in society's service there are 1000 others who are in it for something else. First there is the legion of well-dressed ladies who are putting in their "trousseau two." Those are the two years after graduation from college that are spent in accumulating money for a nice wedding trousseau. Then there is that large crop of females who are mainly in service to their husbands. They are "putting him through" law school, medical school, the Ph.D. program, an internship, or his computer specialization program. They see their own careers as completely subservient, secondary, and almost trivial.

Then there is the sad bunch of girls who found neither a husband nor someone to put through law school. They hang around for years taking their own disappointment out on the kids.

Add to this a large group of the upwardly mobile. These come ordinarily from the working classes, are primarily members of minority races, and are racist to the core. Before they whack the kid's behind they make sure he understands it is all to help him see the light. The message is: If I can make it so can you, and if you don't, you make me look bad, so shape up.

The largest group of those "in service to society" are hard-core ritualists, both male and female, who plod along thinking that their jobs are easy compared to most workers. They think about the short hours, the long vacations, the summers off, and a hundred shucks to get the students to do their work for them. They're the ones who give lots of tests and let the kids grade each other as a way of "giving them responsibility." On the blackboards in their classrooms you can see something like this:

Class Assignment
Period 1—Chambers, Basic Grammar: Pages 97–99, Examples 1–115
Period II—Smith, Basic English: Pages 16–18, Examples 1–50
Period III—Same as period I
Period IV—Same as period II

And so on through every period. And this teacher looks up every 15 minutes to see who isn't hard at work, and resents the distraction, because he was right in the middle of an interesting travel article in *Life* magazine.

Of course I am generalizing and most teachers will insist that they do not fall into any of the categories I have mentioned. I have never met a sorority girl who considered herself the typical sorority girl. I am not reporting research. I am just going on heavy experience and a lot of inference. The inference comes from the present state of education: Things just don't get that bad when the majority of personnel are concerned and dedicated.

But I have only discussed one class of helpers. I think that there are two other types. I am now talking about educators on every level of education and every type, public and private. There is the first group which I have just described, the institutional helpers, who are the main body of helping shuckers in the system. Then there are those who have a slightly different shuck going. I'll call them the "real but qualified helpers." I think I belong in this group although I'm trying to work my way out of it.

These are people who go out on a limb for a student, really give him everything they have and then get pissed off when he doesn't take advantage of it, or even worse, when he doesn't become a disciple. We can draw a parallel to our country's position in foreign affairs. We give lots of people lots of money but we take it all back when they don't do things our way. Who are we interested in helping, the leaders or the people? The leaders change but the same people get different treatment. Teachers are often like this with students. What they give is almost always qualified by what they expect in return. In this respect they are just like parents, saying: "I gave you everything and look how you repay me." Even if the kid has the courage of his convictions, he walks around after that with a heavy burden of guilt.

Then there are the unqualified or true helpers, a very rare breed. Unqualified giving or helping is an unrealistic expectation. Human beings in our time and place have learned that this is a give-and-take world. There are not many saints around. But there are some and they deserve our love and gratitude for showing us what is possible in the human spirit. The number of teachers who fall into this last category is small, but they exist, and the number, I believe, is growing. There are beautiful young men and women who are trying to become teachers and are even willing to pass through a school of education to have the chance. But few of them make it into the public schools because they are crucified in the process of trying to get there. They want to help and they will be devoted to children, but they will not be what the Neanderthal student-teaching supervisors and self-righteous master-teachers want to make out of them. They fall by the wayside and the shuckers step in to take their place. And this appears to be the way we want it, at least for now.

The future holds some promise. It promises us a way to give up the helping shuck. It exists in the notion of *open structure,* which is an idea that has gained some popularity in recent days. Open structure means that both the goals of the classroom and the means for attaining them are open. We can choose from a number of alternatives or, hopefully, choose no alternative at all. It is left up to the individual student. The point is, if the teacher does not impose his version of goals and means on students, then he is not forced to evaluate the progress of individuals in any standardized terms. Real help occurs when we help persons do what they want to do, if we can. In these terms we don't have to deceive them into believing we are helping them even when we are punishing them. In open structure we do not need to force kids to do our will, which we say is really best for them, in the name of helping them. If we don't have preset rigid strategies, and we do have open, individually determined goals, then force or punishment becomes irrelevant and we don't have to justify such in shuck terms.

In brief, this is the possibility for the future. Unfortunately, it is not the probability for most students in most places. As an ex-student and now ex-teacher told me the other day, "I think I'll have a couple of babies and wait to see what happens in the schools. By the time I'm ready to go back it might be different." Unfortunately, most of us don't have the time, wherewithal, or luxury just to wait.

CHAPTER THREE

The Morality Shuck

Every school child knows some things are right and some things are wrong. Our morality grows as we come to learn the "no's"; it is the price we pay for avoiding punishment as children. We learn that what is right is what is not wrong. Everybody in our society thinks teachers are true believers. They are the models par excellence of what our society requires us to pretend to be. The teachers do not require of us as children that we also believe; it is enough that our actions be consistent with their expectations. Thus as young children we learn how to live, how to be moral, how to survive and prosper behind this "morality."

In the present sense, there is no difference between a moral rule and a convention: what a culture respects as an acceptable norm or value may be interchanged with a moral at any point. I have not used quotation marks around the word moral because we fully accept the absolute rightness of our conventions. The difference between our conventions and the conventions of other cultures or subcultures is that ours are congruent with fundamental truth, and theirs are considered either "funny" ways of living, or wrong, subnormal, or all three.

Morality issues cause all of us much doubt and anxiety. We are always falling into contradictions which force us to work out acceptable rationalizations. In order to make child rearing easier on ourselves and thus avoid examining these contradictions, we let school teachers and ministers deal with the moral education of our children, while we make fun of their prudery and ignore their precepts and values in our own adult lives. We live comfortably with the overall rationalization—which we then term "reality"—that we are "only human." Being only human is a luxury we reserve for ourselves and deny to teachers as well as to children and religious leaders. Yet, to their everlasting credit, public school teachers assume the burden of virtue selflessly, and carry on beyond our wildest expectations.

There was a time, not so far removed from today, when school teachers were carefully watched in every small town. Female teachers were usually required to live in respectable boardinghouses which did not accept male visitors except on Sunday, attend church regularly, see gentlemen friends under only the most public of circumstances, and never smoke, drink, or say "damn." I personally knew a man who, while working in a small town in Maryland as late as 1960, was having his beer delivered in milk cartons so the trash man wouldn't gossip to parents about the number of beer cans in his trash.

But these proceedings no longer characterize the mainstream of moralism in teachers or in education. Now the evaluation has shifted to serious and meaningful violations of expectations, such as cursing, wearing hair too long or skirts too short, becoming too friendly with students, being responsive to students' feelings about personal matters, or mentioning anything about sex or politics in the classroom.

To take just one of the above, the history of sex in the classroom is fraught with repression. I remember, as a student, how we all froze, blushed, and coughed the day the senior English teacher read from Wordsworth: "she bared her busom to the moon." Students don't blush as much any more. Although they have outgrown this kind of decadent morality, their teachers have not. They are still protecting young minds from falling into smutful associations . . . on the grounds that the students can't handle it, of course.

The last year I was at Cuney High, I worked part time as a counselor. I spent an hour a day in the vice-principal's office, talking to kids who were sent there for disrupting the class, or disrupting the teacher, which seems to be about the same thing. I only got to see boys because it was part of the same morality structure that required us to segregate the sexes every chance we could. The cases I remember best were violations of the language ethic, where some boy had used the word "fuck" to express something he was feeling rather than to repress his feelings, swallow his words, and raise his hand to make a formal statement. I was never sure whether it was the morality dealing with cursing or with sex that was being invoked. At any rate, nobody was really dealing with it in the classroom, on either level. All I could do was say that I didn't personally think it was so bad, but that it was a violation of a school rule and I was therefore required to assign detentions. You'd have thought I was in training to become a school administrator.

The alternative to repressing the language of children is (1) to accept it and (2) to build upon it. In the abstract anybody who has ever thought of teaching knows about this process. But when it comes to "dirty" words, the moral issue seems to outweigh the educational one.

The reason that most teachers in most places are afraid to accept what the kids say, although they personally (I believe) can handle it, is that (1) it might lead to other things which they can't handle and (2) it might get out among the public and jeopardize their jobs. I would suggest that those who are marginally open to letting kids be themselves consider that, for most kids, life is so segregated that parents never hear about what they are doing anyhow, and those "other things" have their own rationale. The thing that group leaders have discovered is that if persons can say "fuck" as much as they want they don't often feel they have to say it. Also, if it is part of the acceptable vocabulary, as it is on the street, then it is not disruptive every time it comes up. Teachers had better take heed that the culture is changing and unless they plan to use bleeps they must realize that one of the prime associates of culture change is language change. Those who are not in favor of holding back cultural change had better practice saying "fuck" in public.

The conception of morality held by most educators has very little to do with many of the important philosophical statements on ethics that have come down through the years from wise men—for example, "do unto others," or "liberty, equality, fraternity." The educational systems are locked into conventions; in order to change them, it would require a vast overhaul of our entire social structure.

The point is that we organize our classes with the teacher's authority as paramount. Thus any disrespect for that authority is judged as a violation of classroom morality. If this were not the case, kids would be allowed to be equal to teachers in responsibility, power, and influence, and that would require that we figure out entirely new ways of working in schools. Rather than take the risk of having to adjust to whatever change this would bring, we continue to judge students on the basis of how well they accept the authority of teachers and thus how moral and good they are because they fit in.

In sociological jargon, morality is simply being well socialized, knowing when to do what and when not to do it. There's nothing basically spiritual or conscious or individual about it, for it's just a matter of figuring out what others expect and giving it to them. Immorality turns out to be a violation of the expectations of the school's power structure and it can happen in any area of school life. Later in life, immorality still means not meeting the expectations of others, whether the others are clearly defined or just the ambiguous and threatening "they"—the corporate state, the officials, the neighbors, the relatives. That booming social no-no can condition even the way we hold our bodies or choose life's work.

Now this is straight and obvious sociology. Where does the shuck come in? It comes in best through the eyes of the students who see through shuck games very clearly. In a story-writing class in senior English, George wrote a descriptive account of his experiences at the school. His words express the games far better than I ever could—he was a victim of those games.

As I have said before, George was my favorite student. Of all the humans I experienced during my five years at Cuney High, George was the most memorable. He was a real person, who was always staggering from the blows he encountered just trying to survive at the school. Through it all, he managed to keep some perspective on the values of those around him and never became completely captured by anyone or by any one way. I expect, or perhaps I should say I'd like to think, I had a decent influence on him: I kept him writing. What follows is part of his best effort. I'll use other pieces of his writing in other sections of this book.

Of all the students I taught in senior English, he was the one I most trusted with my personal wish that he write in his own language, and not shy away from the truth or from truthful expression of what he saw and felt, including the use of "dirty words." My faith was rewarded. He used language, including bad language, well and honestly, where it belonged.

5th Period

A TEACHER TO REMEMBER

George Sardowski
B12 English
Mr. Weinberg

Mr. Moody, I remember him best because I had him twice, once with the College Prep kids and the next time with the kids from Industrial Arts. They were very different kids and to tell you the truth I like the ones from Industrial Arts best because they weren't phonies. All kids cheat a little bit in tests, I've seen it, but the kids from College Prep always got away with it because the teacher trusted them more, but if someone like James (a nonachieving, working-class kid)* came up with an A on a test he got marked down for cheating even if the teacher didn't catch him. After awhile you learn just how good the teacher thinks you are and so when you cheat you don't do much better than they expect you can do. The College Prep kids who know their work don't let you copy off it like the ones in Industrial Arts do. Of course, not many of the kids in Industrial Arts know that much so you wouldn't want to take a chance in copying off them, except for maybe somebody like Tom Dealy He would never hide his paper from anybody and when I got to be friends with him it was very helpful, if I was lazy or something. Teachers have the whole thing figured out wrong though, because if you get caught cheating off a kid's paper when you're in the Industrial Arts class the teacher always knows that the kid whose paper you're copying off is also cheating by letting you. When you get caught in College Prep classes the kid whose paper you're looking at is always innocent as a lamb, and that sure isn't true.

Even though it was much tougher in College Prep classes in English with Mr. Moody, it was a lot more interesting. At least there he would let kids talk a little bit if he was sure they were going to say

*My parentheses.

the right thing, but in my other class with him we'd sit quiet most of the time figuring out hundreds of words in hundreds of sentences to see if they were verbs or adjectives and interesting stuff like that. You can only do so much of that crap without getting very bored but the way Mr. Moody talked you'd think he was letting us have the best experience of our lives. He would walk up and down the aisle straightening his tie and checking to see if we were doing it and sometimes he'd walk around for the whole period and nobody would say nothing until somebody cracked and threw down his pencil like he'd had enough and then Mr. Moody would give out with the crap about how this kid who couldn't take it any longer was going to end up a ditch digger and did he think digging ditches was going to be more interesting than doing grammar?

At least five kids would shout out "yes" at the same time and Mr. Moody would really get on us then. He'd assign another five pages of the same crap for homework and told us to start thinking about the future and about how it was no fun breaking your back ten hours a day for $45 a week. I don't know how he thought he knew.

We had these little reddish brown grammar books that we'd work out of every day and the books were very crummy which I think is one reason why we figured grammar was very crummy. I guess they were printed in about 1890 or something but Mr. Moody thought they were good enough for us. He really didn't have much respect for our class, especially the girls who he used to insult all the time. He would really pick on the girls who were in the beauticians course but he would do it in a way that you were never really sure he was meaning it about you. Like he would say things like some people don't really have to work hard to get ahead, they can just make themselves attractive with all sorts of disguises and get some man who thinks it's really them beneath the crud.

There was nothing that burned Mr. Moody up as much as some girl combing her hair or putting on makeup in class. That made him really wig and he didn't care what we were doing, he would stop and give us all a half hour talk on manners, and it was always the same crap over and over again. It was sure different in the College Prep classes. It almost never got lectures on manners.

I don't think putting makeup on in class is a great thing or anything, but I sure can't see anybody getting so burned up as Mr.

Moody did. You'd think somebody set fire to his precious grammar books or something. But he had a terrible hatred for girls who weren't serious about their work, especially if they were the kind of girls who wore a lot of makeup and teased their hair and maybe bleached it too. And it was even worse on them if they were well built and wore tight sweaters. I'll never forget Milly Montgomery and Mr. Moody as long as I live. He really had it in for her and she gave it back tit for tat and I mean that.

She wore very tight sweaters and always held her breath when she walked into English class just to bug old Moody, like we sometimes called him. He would always pretend not to be particularly interested but you could tell he was fighting not to look. She was a very tall girl too and wore her hair very high so you couldn't miss her. She was also one who would put on makeup in class just to bug him. I think she would rather hear him talk about proper behavior than do grammar so she did it often. Besides, she liked to fight back with him which always made it interesting for the rest of us, especially if we were marking verbs and pronouns.

He always made her stand up when he was talking to her. So she went along with it and she would put her hands on her hips and throw her body way out and keep shifting her hips. Some of the guys in the class would whistle at her and that really got her going and started Mr. Moody giving out detentions left and right. Mr. Moody would always start out very sarcastic with her. He asked her if she thought it would help her in her profession if she could read and write.

"You have to sign checks," she said, "and I can do that."

"Oh," he said, "You expect to make a good deal of money, do you?"

"I think I'll find it somewhere," she said smiling at the rest of us and we all gave a laugh.

"What will you be giving in return for all this wealth?" he asked but he shouldn't have, except that he really didn't know any better.

"Nothing you could use," she said and that really ground out the class.

He tried not to look upset but you could tell she was getting to him, "I certainly couldn't," he said, "I've always believed in quality products."

That bugged Milly but she wasn't about to let him know he'd

gotten to her either, so she said, getting a smile out first and winking at one of the other girls she sat in the back with, "I don't know what you're thinking about Mr. Moody, but I'm talking about giving permanent waves."

"What's the use," he said. He was always saying that. "Sit down and get back to work, you can't make a silk purse out of a sow's ear. I wonder why I try." It was one of his favorite sayings.

He could really make you feel small with his what's the use sayings but it didn't bother most people, like Milly or James, but it got to me. It made it very tough for someone like me who wanted to get out of there and back into College Prep because he figured that we just weren't interested in doing anything right so he wouldn't give you a chance to. But I kept trying.

I'd wait around until after class when everyone was going so it wouldn't look like I was trying to brown nose, and then I'd go up and tell him that I thought that he was right in telling off those people who were messing around, especially Milly, and could I do something to make up for the time we missed because I was really interested in doing good in the class. I figured I'd tried everything else so I had nothing to lose.

It might have worked except that he started asking me to do things in class which wouldn't have been too much to do, like taking messages and stuff, except that if I did it the rest of the class would have really put me down and I didn't want that as much as I wanted to get out of the class. So one time I told him my feet were killing me and the class liked it but he got bugged and never asked me again. I guess I just wasn't smart enough to play it both ways like some kids.

Most of the kids thought it was OK to cheat if you were just trying to pass a course because nobody wanted anybody else to flunk but if you were cheating to get an "A" that was lousy.

There was no sense cheating in the classes I was in after I was Industrial Arts, because nobody knew anything anyhow and nobody ever studied and besides I knew almost everything they asked on tests but was having trouble getting good grades anyhow. That's because the teachers we had always had a lot of different ways to figure out what your grade was besides the scores you got on tests. Mr. Moody always thought it was very important to be neat and if you did neat papers he'd figure out another way to get you. He didn't have to with me, because I never did things neatly but some others did. He'd get them on something, like how did they cooperate or how much extra credit did they do.

One last thing about Mr. Moody was that if he really got to like you then you could do no wrong. He would overlook almost anything, except maybe criticizing him. There was this one student who he liked a lot who never did a grammar lesson the whole time I was in class. Moody never mentioned it. Then one time, for some dumb reason this guy raised his hand and politely said that he thought doing grammar was a waste of time especially if you were going to be an engineer like he was. That was the last time he ever got away with not doing grammar. He should have known better.

In case you'd like your interpretations classified, here is my list of a few major moralistic shucks imbedded in George's paper. You may perceive more.

1. Violations of the morality code are interpreted differently for kids with different social statuses. (For example, smoking in the bathroom is cause for expulsion of a vocational student, but leads to a lecture on health if the offender is college prep honors.)
2. When teachers tell you it is intrinsically good to work hard, they really mean to keep busy so you don't bother them.
3. When teachers convince you it is moral to have high aspirations, they are really asking you to have a stake in getting somewhere. Otherwise, how can they use taking it away as a threat?
4. Being moral for a girl is playing down your sex or your femininity because the teacher (either male or female) can't handle it.
5. Morality is acting as if the class members, including yourself, were sexual neuters.
6. Morality is controlling your desire to express yourself when you are turned on, whether it be in whistling at girls or in enjoying a lesson.
7. Morality is volunteering to help the teacher with administrative chores rather than to do the classwork, and betraying your own sense of propriety and values to get ahead with the teacher—like agreeing with him when you really don't.
8. Morality is cheating to survive but not prevail.

9. Morality is turning in papers that are not messy, as if this said anything about your mind or manners.
10. Morality is a matter of being personally liked by the teacher.
11. Morality is being bright and inquisitive if you're in the college prep course and quiet, passive, and easily disciplined if you're in industrial arts.
12. Morality is meeting the expectations of the teacher, even if it means lowering your own aspirations, so the teacher won't have to reevaluate your work or effort or defend you to the administrators.

A number of years ago a sociologist named Becker wrote up a study which illustrated the point that teachers don't like students who are dirty, who curse, or who act with sexual awareness. The kids they did like were those who were well trained to control their feelings.

Teachers play a fundamental role in helping us develop our morality. It starts out something like this:

In a second-grade classroom, Tommy and Fred are swinging wildly at each other. Their faces are livid, their eyes intense. Then they are on the floor rolling over and over, punching, squeezing, screaming.

Tommy feels a firm hand lifting him up, pulling him off. Then Fred feels another hand holding him away. They are suddenly aware that they have been intercepted by the teacher, but they don't care yet. Their anger is too high, they try to reach out to the enemy for one more punch.

"I'll kill the bastard," Fred yells, straining to break from Mrs. Smith's hold.

"Now, that will be enough," Mrs. Smith says, loud and firm. "Don't you know where you are?" She shakes the two kids to a settled standoff. Their breathing slows down.

"Now, let's get to the bottom of this," says the the well-meaning teacher. "Let's go over here, sit down and calmly talk it over." She leads the two boys to a bench across the room. She sits between them.

"Well, now, what was it all about?"

Fred starts pointing a mean finger, "That motha fucker stole my. . . ."

"Hold it, hold it," Mrs. Smith intervenes, "we do not use that kind of language in the classroom." She points a threatening finger at both of them. "Now, once more, remembering where you are, in your own words, tell me what happened."

So there we have it. Tommy and Fred are told that it is not right to express their feelings with their bodies, nor is it appropriate to use certain words to communicate their feelings. They learn that lack of control in the classroom will get them into trouble. Further, they learn that the way to solve problems is to talk about them, in a nice, polite tone, which is really only possible long after the feelings have dissipated. Teachers push us to develop nice sounding abstract concepts to substitute for basic, feeling words, in order to help us appear both moral and intelligent.

Now, if we return to Tommy and Fred and Mrs. Smith, we find two dirty boys who've just been told their feelings are not appropriate in the classroom. And, in addition, they are two boys who now have a reputation for cursing, fighting, and allowing themselves to get dirty. Given what we know about how teachers form moralistic judgments, should this behavior persist, even at wide intervals, this reputation, acquired in only the second grade, will follow the boys throughout much of their school career. It will be reported to the "office" and become part of the childrens' records—gradually teachers will come to expect and actually provoke a similar behavior—and the child may even begin to accept this expectation. Soon what was once an attempt to defend oneself honestly and feelingly will become a self-fulfilling prophesy of rebellious behavior and language.

The measure of self-control that children in most school settings are expected to exhibit would tax most adults to the breaking point. Children are screamed at, insulted, hit, embarrassed, demeaned, rejected, judged, made to sit quietly for hours, and lectured to endlessly on the right way to behave. And there is nothing they can do about it without being immoral. If they scream, fight, leave the room without permission, talk back, laugh, or cry, they are punished, and the more they are punished, the more they become defined as basically immoral youngsters. Those not capable of such inhuman control are selectively weeded out, isolated, and allocated to the failure road. Millions of decent, active, honest, and enthusiastic youngsters begin their trek down this pathway every year.

The virtue, then, is self-control. And in the name of self-control, children are restrained from being children, prevented from feeling and from being human. The solution, of course, requires that we dissolve the notion that self-control is intrinsically virtuous, at least in areas where children are not a threat to each other's well-being. To say that self-control is a valuable training in other areas is a shuck in the sense that training is not transferable and the danger of creating a robot is considerable. Eliminating control training means that we take the time, and make the effort, to really see and hear our students, to allow them the full range of emotional outlets, to allow each act to be judged by the group as to its effects upon the group. As teachers, it means we would have to ask ourselves whether or not we restrain behavior solely on the grounds that it violates our personal sense of propriety and makes our jobs more unpredictable and demanding. Merely "being"—sensitively interacting—with other humans is always more taxing than leaning on power and learning to dictate. If we find that we do, indeed, fail to respond to these people as whole human beings with more to them than simply rational brains, our entire manner and attitude toward ourselves as well as to them would have to undergo serious readjustment.

Humanistic educators are constantly arguing for an environment in which children are permitted a wide range of emotional or affective outlets. The assumption here is simply that it is healthy for children to live without the ever-present, totally repressive fear that one of their feelings is about to run away with them, which will lead to dire punishment and a falling from grace. A second assumption is that it might also be healthy for teachers, who will thus be allowed to relate to human beings all day long, rather than to animals, criminals, or sex fiends. If we could begin with the notion that children are quite eager to learn and able to be cooperative and respectful of the feelings and needs of others without punitive rules, then we would be one step closer to making the classroom a human, natural environment in which *all*, including the teacher, can experience growth.

But the big question the shuck inspector must ask in this regard is whether or not the self-control expectation is related to some worthy state of being in itself or turns out to be just another strategy for controlling the behavior of children. That is, is it good to exhibit "self-control," or is it just *useful* to us as teachers? An even more poignant question follows: Do we require others to exhibit self-control because we are ourselves unable to handle our emotions and the emotions of others? Much of the issue of the morality shuck hinges upon the answer to this question.

If we are totally capable of allowing persons to express their emotions, and yet decide it is of some benefit to the group to incorporate rules against such spontaniety, that is another matter. Then we must only question what is really of "benefit" to the group. Personally, I have been persuaded, through many years of close contact with school teachers, that too many of them are unable to handle the emotionality of anyone, much less children. Teachers often personify the virtue structure of the entire society, and in that society, most of us walk and talk past each other in absolute terror of honesty or the genuine expression of feeling.

No wonder the film *Love Story* was so enormously successful: in the dark protection of the movie theater we can sit and feel. It is practically the only place except the bedroom where many persons allow themselves to feel any emotion in the presence of others.

The new thinking is that the only way you can help some children, mainly those from minority community schools, to learn is to let them be themselves from the beginning of their education; that is, to bring the world of the streets into the classroom and build upon it. This has been the message of a great many important books which have influenced teachers in public schools as well as those who have moved to free schools, where the problem doesn't exist in the same way. The culture of the school with respect to conventional moralities was so thrown into question that innovations have been possible. I have seen some public schools where kids write compositions that I would have classified as pornographic, but they get to write. I have also seen many teachers encourage kids to yell and cry and shout for joy, and in these situations there was a lot less shouting done than in many classrooms where emotions were strictly taboo. Kids will fight back any way they can, unless they don't feel they have to. This solves both the institutional problem and the psychological one that is produced by repressed emotionalism.

There are a few areas of campus morality where shuck games are played out, but on the whole higher education has a different ethical structure than that of the elementary or high school. There, control of student behavior is based more on competition and evaluation of achievement rather than morality. Most campus administrators, though there are significant exceptions, do not usually play the role of parents: students can smoke, drink, wear what they please, study or not study as they wish, and be as unindustrious and/or dirty as they desire. For the most part, college professors do not flinch when a student drops a "fuck" or "bullshit" into the discussion. Nor do they get uptight if some coed starts massaging the neck muscles of the boy in front of her. Nevertheless, administrators still attempt to control behavior on campus through three general areas of concern, namely, sexual behavior, cheating, and respect for property.

In my opinion the sexual issue is trivial but it springs up now and again, in true shuck fashion, when somebody makes a fuss. Then everybody, who couldn't care less in their own knowledge of the dirty business, suddenly acts very shocked and outraged. On my own campus, about three years ago, a story hit the papers that teaching assistants in the Italian Department were trading grades for encounters with female students. Nobody ever really specified the exact behavior being bartered, but everybody snickered. There followed a grand investigation behind closed doors, and it was all resolved somehow. Gradually the noise calmed down. The campus paper published a few interesting letters to the editor, and a couple of debates ensued, which most of us enjoyed. One of my colleagues wrote a letter about how the assistants were really communicating an important quality of the Italian character to students, and how better to educate them than by example. A few humorless Italian-American students condemned the letter as misrepresenting Italian morality, and so it went.

The shuck behind it, as I indicated, had to do with the basis on which the judgments were made: not because of any sexual behavior involved, but because the wrong person found out. As far back as I can remember, first as a student and then as a member of the faculty, I was aware of goings on between faculty and faculty, faculty and students, teaching assistants and students, and even (on one occasion) a high-ranked administrator and a graduate student. It's no big thing, right? Except of course if daddy finds out and complains, especially if he's the friend of a governor or a state senator.

Cheating and plagiarism still remain important issues. I have no idea how many college students do a little or a lot of either. I would suspect, knowing the student role as well as I do, that a great deal more goes on than ever comes to light. I suspect students spend as much time preparing to cheat as they would if they just studied for the exam or wrote the paper. I also expect that cheating, like the sex business, is something most faculty would rather ignore unless somebody makes a point of it. I have known some faculty, however, who are terribly paranoid when it comes to term papers, and even some who enjoy catching offenders. Recognizing on some level that their classes are intrinsically uninteresting to students, they can't believe anyone would do the kind of work they expect. But the prevailing morality remains—despite the fact that the task is both uninteresting and of no particular value to students—a matter of "since I had to do it, so should he," especially on the graduate level.

In large classes it is awfully hard to match term papers with any knowledge of the students' abilities. I am sure many students operate on that knowledge, turning papers in which are far above their level of motivation for research or their writing ability. I also know student groups have networks of papers which are available for either copying or reworking.

My experience with some students has been that, once they become willing to cheat at all, they are not interested in holding back, which means making any part of it their own work. The most they are willing to do is change the title page, which contains the name of the person who originally wrote the paper.

One of my colleagues returned a term paper with the comment "This is an 'A' paper. It was an 'A' paper when John Smith wrote it and it is an 'A' paper when you wrote it." I once made a practice of keeping term papers for a period of three years and if I saw one I remembered I would do something about it. Students don't usually turn a copied paper into the same professor who had assigned it originally. I no longer assign them to undergraduates and know graduate students well enough to recognize the work so I am not caught in the moral dilemma of punishing or questioning students for cheating on a paper my teaching could in no way motivate them to want to write for themselves.

I'm sure a great deal of cheating goes on in college. I really don't feel bad about that, but I do feel bad that it has to happen. If students are in college to be sorted out and allocated and separated, I can't really see what is so wrong about dealing with absurd demands in a "deviant" way. If college is meant to separate "the men from the boys," if teaching is based on the ethic that I had to do it, so he or she must too, and not on personally motivated searching and some sort of class work truly geared to real life, then why should a student mess up his chances of success by taking the time and going through the pain of learning something? We've set it up in such a way that students in fact do not have the time or the freedom to learn what they want to learn in their way. They well know that they have to make the grades. They tell themselves they'll learn all they want to learn, after they graduate, but with time pressure, and parent pressure, and money pressure, college has become just another environment in which basic survival is the foremost task, and being a real student has usually not proven a valid survival mechanism. I think it is very sad that students are forced to do anything they can to survive the college rat race, but I know that under such conditions I don't blame them when they respond as we demand of them—as well-conditioned caged animals.

Another of the morality issues has to do with special favors or privilege. One ethical theme professors try to follow is to treat all students alike and evaluate them on their performance, not on who they are as persons. In some schools I've heard this principle is violated in favor of athletes, but except for special tutoring and directions to easy classes, this is not true in mine. When I look down at the football game from half a mile up behind the end zone and squint through my binoculars I balance my hostility at such poor treatment of faculty by reminding myself that any athletic department that deals with its faculty this way certainly can't be expecting differential treatment for its athletes.

The only alternative to the problems created by cheating that I could consider would require a complete reorganization of the system of evaluation, discussed in Chapter Ten as "Universalism" and "Unidimensionalism." Behind such shuck words is the consideration that perhaps standards should be different for people with different interests and the same standards should not be applied to every student. I realize this is a very radical proposal but that is only true for the present. The structures for evaluation are changing in most places. We have nongraded classes, pass-no credit classes, and contract-grading classes where students are graded on what they say they will accomplish in areas of their own interest. Good things are coming, committees are at work. Our children will have it easier.

Although the campus differs from the lower grades insofar as much moralistic ritualism is concerned, one area in which it does carry over is in respect for property. Recent events have highlighted where our values really lie, in our respect for property rather than human dignity. As students begin to protest our nation's war crimes and the contribution of higher education to the same, in the only way they feel will be heard, and in the only place in our society where it is possible for them to protest, they find they will pay dearly for their misdemeanors. For every broken window, local police exacted two broken heads. "But," the citizens defended, "what would you do if hoodlems were seeking to destroy your home?"

For me it would depend on whether or not the hoodlems were my own children. I might try to hear their frustrations and their message before I hit them or sent police after them. To whom, in fact, does the campus really belong?

One thing we've learned is that it is not the property of the students who go there. It turns out that the campus, private or public, belongs to the people and the people don't want their windows broken by those who occupy the colleges. No matter. The values were laid down long ago, when young children at small desks were punished severely for writing on them, or for marking books, or for breaking windows, or for using school equipment in their way rather than the teacher's way. Children learn early what adults respect, what authorities respect, what the law respects. That's why they mark up bathrooms and walls and now whole cities, to show their contempt for property. Of course I am only talking about the deviants. The well socialized are now spanking their own children for violations of property. They completely ignore violations of human dignity as children learn the new Golden Rule: "Do others before they do you." After all, "that's the way the world is." Morality lies in an abiding reverence for private property; to me this is one of the most serious perversions of human values known to society, and, of course, to the classroom.

Now, for those who are interested in untangling the moralistic shuck, here is my advice. We begin with a list of all the acts for which we punish children and we ask ourselves two basic questions: "In what way is it bad for children to do that?" and "In what way is it bad for us to let them do that?" Let's make a sample list and undertake the exercise.

1. Cursing

2. Writing on desks
3. Boys peeping into the girls' bathroom
4. Handing in messy, dirty papers
5. Speaking without permission

Now, we have to admit on the face of it that none of these behaviors is intrinsically injurious to the child. They only become his problem because others do not appreciate what he is doing. So we come to a more precise conception of a student's problem: he has a problem when we disapprove of what he does.

Our other question is, "In what way is it bad for children to do that?" We can begin by saying that it is bad because it violates our rules and without our rules we would descend into chaos. Now we know this is illogical, because doing away with one rule that prevents chaos doesn't stop us from replacing it with another rule that might serve the same function while being a lot less harmful to the subjects of the rules. This argument forces us to look precisely into the real basis for the rule.

Cursing: We have rules against cursing because cursing is not nice.

Writing on desks: We have this rule because we want children to grow up with respect for property, particularly if the property belongs to someone who happens to own a lot more of it than we do.

Peeping into the girls' bathroom: This is to maintain the sanctity and mystery of the division of the sexes. On no grounds should boys and girls get to know each other and be comfortable with each other, come what may. After all, the sexes get along so well as a result of our segregationist policies! Also, marriage based on these assumptions is obviously a stable institution indeed.

Handing in a messy, dirty paper: We punish this behavior on the grounds that messy is hard to read and dirt is the carrier of germs and cause of illness. Here we basically try to teach students neat habits because that's what is respected "outside" and our job is to train children to get along in that "real world." According to this argument we should also train children to call oppression love and repression freedom, to cherish our subtle racisms, to lie, cheat, betray, ignore poverty, distrust one another, and so forth, because that's the way it is, "out there." Oh, yes, we do this, too.

Speaking without permission: This is cause for punishment because it retards the progress of the class, holds others up, or perhaps, in some cases, prevents us from accomplishing our goals. If you take a good look behind this shuck, you find yourself asking who really gets held up and from going where? For the kinds of goals most teachers set for their classes, any derailing would be seen as a benefit to the kids. Whose goals are they, after all? I have worked with students of all ages without the "ask for permission to speak" rule, and find if the task and goals are their own they will have no desire to get in each other's ways, or my way as I move to assist them.

This does not mean, of course, that all rules are bad. They are necessary and useful, but only as they are generated to accomplish specific tasks, by the people who want to accomplish these tasks. Thus what we must crush in formal education is the notion that some virtues are right and eternal in and of themselves, regardless of their effect on children, and shift to a concern for establishing rules or structures that help us function and grow in our work. The claim that conventional school virtues are anything more than blind faith in tradition is a monumental shuck. As humanistic teachers concerned with maximizing the potential of all children, regardless of training, we must confront these moralistic shucks, even at the cost of our "morality."

CHAPTER FOUR

The Status Shuck

The status shuck is the blood and bones of the educational shucking game. Its skeleton roams the width and breadth of educational life, converting love for learning into a battlefield strewn with the bodies of the losers and the egos of the winners. Its sense of direction has little to do with souls—which are either destroyed or lost in the process of achieving status.

It runs on standards. In the larger society it is a standard of living buttressed by the several components of status: money, education, and occupation. In the school, status revolves around grades and academic rewards, participation in the many prestigious activities like football, student government, and the so-called friendship groups such as clubs, fraternities, and cliques. From the school's point of view status is achievement; from the students' perspective it is popularity.

A status shuck is anything a student does to convince anyone he is better than everybody else. Anything a principal does to convince anyone that his school is better than any other is a status shuck. Anything a teacher does to convince a student that he needs to do well in school to get ahead of the next guy is a status shuck.

Parents get into the game heavily. Whether it be by acts as obvious as buying a child a book about a medical doctor to convince the child that he should become one too, or as subtle as becoming an anxious parent if the child shows no interest in reading before starting school. It is all part of the same shuck. Symptomatic of the competitive, middle-class life from which it all comes and to which it all goes, the name of the game is show. It doesn't matter if the kid is an idiot, or if he is totally unhappy, just so long as he learns to look good. Mothers dress their little girls in pink dresses with white lace, curl their hair, and scrub them pink so teachers will be sure to notice how nice they are. Being nice is worth from one to two full grades on the A to F grading system.

At PTA meetings, parents and teachers get the opportunity to shuck one another, to convince each other they are giving more than they do, and to lie to each other about the kids. Parents used to tell me their kids spent several hours a day doing homework when I knew they didn't even take their books home. And I used to tell them their kid was smart if he was just normal, that he was trying if he was slow witted, and that he meant well and would be a good, hard-working citizen if he was illiterate.

Middle-class parents play the game pretty seriously. When I taught in the ghetto I had very few complaints about not giving the kids much homework. Over in the suburbs, parents would frequently come in and complain that the kids weren't being given enough work to help them do well on the college boards, or to help them learn the discipline that would be required to assure good enough grades to get them into medical school or law school.

Everybody wants his kid to do better than the next kid. Nobody thinks much about the cost. But the truth of it is that everybody pays, dearly. No one comes out of the status game with much left in him; outside him, things look better—he has his prizes and laurels and transcripts. Parents have that special kind of myopia that makes it impossible for them to generalize the cost to others, especially to their own kids. When one college student shoots himself in the dormitory bathroom, everybody thinks he was mentally disturbed. Nobody thinks about the forces operating on his own child to do the very same thing.

The status shuck does have its funny sides, though, if you enjoy laughing at feeble attempts to be something you're not. I used to laugh a lot at kids who tried to speak good English, trying to convince me they were really A students despite the F's on their tests. It always sounded like a bad play in which nobody really believed in the part he was playing. Later, when these same students, or slightly brighter versions, got into college, they would come around with the same shuck, only this time it wasn't so funny. The humor ran out when the game got costly and failure to bring off your shuck could be the difference between graduating or being drafted.

The status shucks vary in fairly predictable ways. Boys like to pull the "need at least a B to keep my deferment" shuck, and blacks and browns always need a good grade to get a degree in order to go back to the ghetto to help their people. Waspy females sold themselves on the grounds of their abiding interest in everything. They were always coming around to mention a book they had seen (not read) or to tell me how much they enjoyed the course. Radical students would shuck out on the grounds of working 50 hours a week for the movement.

How things change in short periods! Nine years ago when I taught my first college class the students used to tell me that they couldn't do the work because the frat or sorority demanded so much of their time.

Pseudo-hippie students pull their shuck in a sort of half-hearted manner. They are still well enough trained in the shuck game to try, but their heads are in a different enough place so that they don't really care if you don't believe them. Their shuck is the fact that they are "doing their own thing." If their "own thing" and my "own thing" happened to come together, they would make out fine, but if they didn't, it didn't really matter. Nobody worried much about the outcome.

The popularity shuck is pretty vicious in and of itself, but the school does its best to maximize the effects. In the early grades teachers make little pets out of the cute nice kids and cut the poorly mannered ones quickly out of the game. Everybody wants to be friends with the teacher's favorite on a "maybe some of it will rub off" basis, and nobody wants any dealings with the unwashed untouchable, for the same reason.

Little kids learn the *pulley effect* quickly. If you can't beat the others out by being better, then find a way to pull them down below you. I watched this kind of thing take place while observing some playground activity at the university elementary school. The boys were playing kick ball in one corner of the yard while the girls were all off at the other end trying to hustle the teacher. One of the better players kicked the ball beyond the playing field and it rolled into a little wooded gully at the other end.

They all stood looking down in the gully wondering what to do. It was clear they did not have permission to go there, but since the teacher was so far away it would take half the game to go to her and have her get the ball. So they talked the boy who had kicked it into retrieving it. No sooner was his little head out of sight than three boys rushed off to tattle on him.

It goes on all the time in the classroom. In the lower grades are the kids telling the teacher on each other, and beating up the effeminate kid who knows all the answers and gets 100 on his tests. It takes a slightly different form in high school. High school kids think it's OK to cheat to pass but the cheating is wrong if you cheat to get an A (ask George). This usually means the top kids don't mind too much if somebody just wants to survive, but when survival means threatening their own status at the top of the class, it becomes unethical.

On the college campus the status shuck often takes the form of social distance between professors and students. Students learn early the shuffle and squirm of waiting outside a professor's door, awaiting passage into the grim office and the disinterested face. How do you tell a guy like that you don't understand what he's been saying all semester and a mid-term is coming up? How do you say it and still maintain the illusion that you are college material?

The evaluation system, as we know it, is responsible for the fact that students define each other as competitors, which is why even the best of friends sometimes have fallings out. I know for a fact that many student friends withhold from each other during study sessions, saving that one little bit of information that will make the difference in the score. I've heard businessmen frequently say, "Sure, he's my friend, but business is business." And grades are grades.

How we can turn this all around and build an evaluation system that would preclude a "me against the world" psychology is a rough problem. When you look at the structural components to be overhauled in Chapter Ten you may get some clues as to alternatives. Right now the picture is bleak in most places but, again, there are hopeful signs. As I've said before there are schools which do away with grading and attempt to individualize performance in such a way as to pit every student against his own expectations or his own private contract. There are some colleges which have shifted large parts of the credit system to a pass-no credit evaluation, and there are many individual classes where group projects constitute a good part of the grade, where working together and encouraging others to do their best becomes the norm. Of course, it's still done for all the wrong reasons but at least it's a start.

Before I learned how to allow students to relax and be people, I noticed that everything a student said in my office sounded rehearsed. It probably was. I suspect the same game goes on in most professor's offices. Nobody ever gets to know who the other person really is because we are all so absorbed in our little status games. I remember once being told that this game had a certain value but I forget what it was. I think it had something to do with respect.

Our supervising teachers still tell our female teachers to wear dresses and hose when the entire female subculture is in pants, and rarely wear hose with dresses or skirts. The way one earns respect is to look like something rather than to be someone. This kind of Neanderthal-level twentieth-century thinking permeates the public schools. But a moral can be gleaned from it. When an institution is absolutely bankrupt on the prestige ladder, it does what a businessman in the same boat would do; that is, it tries to look prosperous. A man's status in our society has evolved to an evaluation of position, of appearance.

One does not keep a job by good teaching, one achieves status by getting the job and keeps it by wearing a dress or a suit and tie.

When it becomes impossible to judge quality of teaching we stop expecting it, and when it becomes impossible to win the respect of students by the kind of men and women we are, we feel that we have the right to demand it on the grounds of our appearance or our academic titles.

Last year I went to the graduation ceremonies at our university and sat near the medical student contingent. As usual, they received the greatest applause from the audience. Mothers were in tears and girl friends were seeing visions of sugar plum fairies and Beverly Hills homes with swimming pools. At the end of the fiasco, the medical students went around calling each other "doctor," succeeding in making all the other black-robed students feel just a little inferior. Everyone seemed to have forgotten the words of the bearded Peace Corps bound valedictorian, who had said "we must now go out into the world and make it the kind of world where all men can approach all other men, from the standpoint of trust and equality, and ask for mutual respect and love. If we cannot then we are doomed to fight each other to the death for the highest rung of the ladder."

Can we begin by calling ourselves "doctor"?

On the afternoon before the evening PTA meeting, my old principal Frederich Trope called a special teachers' meeting. The students were dismissed early.

I considered that the meeting must have been important for Trope to give the students an hour off. Later I remarked to one of the PE teachers that Trope must have something big to discuss to be willing to deprive the kids of something they might need to get into college.

He asked, "Which student is that?" We joked about our low status as a college prep school.

I sat in the back of the auditorium next to the coach and waited for the meeting to begin. The coach was describing an incident on the playground, but I wasn't listening. I was thinking about my own standards and expectations. I never thought I would be fighting to get Shakespeare out of the curriculum.

A week before, I had sent Trope a note requesting a curricular change in senior English, from *Romeo and Juliet* to Lorraine Hansberry's *Raisin in the Sun,* the story of a black family's attempt to make it in the white man's world. Trope answered that he didn't think just because the school was changing its racial composition, that this was a reason to lower standards. So I taught *Romeo and Juliet* the best I could, but the class would not get itself in the mood and I couldn't put them there. I remember these thoughts because they plagued me throughout the whole meeting.

The principal pounded on the lectern. "I called you together this afternoon to tell you what I think the purpose of our PTA meeting is tonight."

"How it had better be," the coach whispered in my ear. Everyone knew that the setup for the big fraud was coming.

"We are not meeting with the parents," Trope continued, "to tell them their children can't read or spell or understand anything," he paused. "Not tonight. This evening is a social evening. We will have tea and coffee and cookies and joke with each other and listen to their concerns. We want to make them welcome as visitors and guests. We want to show them what high standards we have for their children, the books we use, the subjects we study."

"They won't understand them any more than their kids," whispered the coach.

"But at least only the well-mannered ones will show up," I said.

I was thinking back to the last PTA meeting. Trope ran one every semester. This was my second, and I dreaded this one as much as I had the first. I did look forward to going out with a few of the other teachers for some drinks to buck ourselves up for the occasion. I suppose many teachers get loaded before PTA meetings.

As Trope whined on in monotonous fashion about how ours was a quality school with high standards and how it was our job to communicate this, I thought about how idiotic was the whole scene. I knew, and others knew, that the parents would be there to put on a show for us and they couldn't care less about what the teachers were doing. It was just a way for conscientious parents to prove to themselves and their kids that they were interested in their children's education. I knew very well, from just one earlier experience, that the ones who would show up would not be the ones that needed to talk and be talked to.

The evening came and there were no surprises. I held a demonstration of my Romeo and Juliet unit and the parents acted like the students, and they played the game out for each other's sakes. After the demonstration the parents in their church clothing wandered around the room inspecting the books that bored their children, and the pictures on the bulletin board that I had gotten from a big file the principal kept for special occasions.

I then talked to them, one family at a time. I knew some facts, for example, that 75 percent of the kids in our school came from broken homes and most of the visitors were from still-intact families. We shook hands formally, and the parents asked all the right questions in polite ways and I gave the right answers. I stood suit to suit with the fathers and they told me what a fine opportunity the particular child was having at Cuney High. We talked about the child's planning to go to college and how they were going to stand behind the child financially.

Things would always be going well in the old man's business. (It was amazing how many had their own businesses.) I accepted the lies, just as they would seem to accept mine. I could sympathize with their need to present a good image, and saw no reason why they shouldn't give back as much bullshit as they were getting.

Later we all gathered in the cafeteria for beverages and cake. Everybody acted as if tea were the strongest beverage they would consider drinking. I stood with the younger teachers, comparing notes on the evening. We had to keep ourselves from breaking into wild laughter at the pretenses we were part of and I was sure many of the parents were doing the same thing.

Then Trope gave his highlight of the evening chat and teachers and parents alike smiled and nodded. Trope had on a new suit for the occasion, and a silk tie. I remember this because every other day he wore an old gray suit and a black linen tie.

"I want to thank you all for being here tonight."

As if we had a choice, I thought.

"I want to say before you all go home . . ."

or to some bar.

". . . that the teachers of Roger Cuney share with me in thanking you for making this evening the success that it always is. As long as parents such as you are able to join the kind of fine staff that we have here . . ."

I thought about the shaggy rejects that staffed the school. Less than half of us even had credentials, and over a quarter were first-year teachers.

". . . in making this the kind of school that it is, with standards that are as high here as anywhere, we do not have to fear a weakening of those standards."

The vice-principal started the applause. It was less than hearty.

"Now," Trope went on, gathering some notes in front of him, "I want to present you with a few facts about your school."

The parents looked on in feigned interest.

"First of all, in a recent survey, 25 percent of our students here at Roger Cuney have declared their intention to go to college, with another 30 percent unsure."

There was a buzzing around the room.

"You can imagine the amount of pressure this puts on our fine teachers."

On he went with a long list of facts about the backgrounds of the teachers. He introduced three new teachers, pointing out their fine academic records. He introduced me for the second time this year. "Mr. Weinberg has a master's degree in English literature," he said proudly.

I smiled awkwardly. Fine lot of use that is, ladies and gentlemen, I said in my head.

Trope ended with the big statistics of the evening, that in a follow-up study of our students, better than one out of four were either college graduates or were in college. He neglected to point out that it was a ten-year random sample survey and that five years earlier the school was in a Jewish neighborhood. Now it was 60 percent black and changing fast. I was caught in my feelings between disgust at the pretense and dishonesty and confusion about why the whole business couldn't be open and real. Why this unending attempt to maintain an image that, being false, does no one any good and actually prevents us from dealing with the real world we have inside and around us?

On the way out, caught in the darkness and hidden by the crowd, I heard a father say, "That motha fucker sure can lay down the bullshit."

"Of course," I said, brushing by and not looking to see the man's surprised face, "that's how you get to be a principal."

Here is another part of George's continuing narrative on my old high school. You'll remember that he had been counseled into vocational arts when he was a complete misfit there. His teacher was a Mr. Green, who George describes far better than I ever could.

The shop teacher was a man named Mr. Green and he took one look at the paper I was carrying and said, "Christ, another reject." That would have made me feel pretty bad ordinarily, but at the time I figured things would kind of work out once they took another look at those intelligence tests I'd taken.

Mr. Green wasn't a bad guy at all if you didn't let his insulting get you down. His favorite name for kids was dummy. He was always saying things like "OK dummies, pay attention even if you won't understand" or "Come on dummies, pretend you understand the English language."

But you always got the feeling that he was on your side a little bit because he needed you. What I mean by that is that he really wasn't so smart himself, like maybe the English and history teachers, and you kind of got the feeling that he thought they were sissies. He even called Mr. Moody, the English teacher and sponsor of the school paper, a faggot. He was real mad at the time when lots of his boys from homeroom got flunks from Mr. Moody.

He used to get up and give us a speech every time report cards came out and he'd use more "dummies" that day than the rest of the semester put together. But it was just his way of talking.

After a while you could tell that he was really more mad at Mr. Moody than he was mad at us, and that's when he said something like, "What can you expect from a faggot like that." That made us feel better, especially since you could tell that Mr. Green was not just saying it like when he called us "dummies," because this time he had a tight grip on the hammer that he carried around in this blue apron that he used to wear all the time. A guy would learn after a while that when Mr. Green was fooling around with that hammer, it was no time to be fooling around at your bench.

We had benches in the shop with stools instead of desks and chairs and this could make you feel inferior if you thought about it, especially since we always had these wood shavings and wood dust over everything. Right next to my bench was a black kid named James James and Mr. Green would call him Jim Jim but after a while nobody laughed, except when Mr. Green would call the wrong boy Jim Jim. He was always mixing up the names of the black kids in class even though you'd think some names like James James would be pretty damn easy to remember. We had a lot of black kids in our curriculum as a matter of fact and it would always strike me as peculiar that black kids all had the same kind of needs, that could all be met by our industrial arts curriculum. This is the way Mr. Gallo, the counselor saw it and he seemed to have been well prepared and educated in these matters and, besides, he never really made a final decision until he got the report from the psychologist.

Almost all the black kids were in our curriculum except for Samuel Wilson who was the president of our student body and you could tell that Mr. Trope was proud of him by the way he would always put his arm around Samuel's shoulder before introducing him to the students during assembly time.

It seemed that he would keep his arm around Samuel the whole time he was talking and you could tell Samuel got pretty bugged. If you mentioned it to him afterwards Samuel would get this funny ugly look on his face and give you the finger. He would even give the finger to the girls and they thought it was really funny when old Samuel gave it to them but if one of us guys gave them the finger they would pretend we weren't even there.

We had about three boys named Sam in our curriculum but the student body president was always called Samuel. He was elected overwhelmingly, and mainly by the girls. He had very light skin and was considered very attractive by the white girls so they voted for him but I don't think they would date him if he asked.

James James and Mr. Green were always kind of at each other.

Mr. Green was very short and looked even shorter with those blue aprons hanging down from the weight of all those tools he would carry around. James was very tall and very thin so Mr. Green and he would kind of go at it from a distance because I really think Mr. Green was bothered by the fact he was so short.

There was this time Mr. Green had James building a bookcase and James was doing some sanding and scraping and moving kinda slow about it. This got Mr. Green angry because he didn't believe in doing things slow when they could be done fast just as well, so anyhow Mr. Green yells from half way across the room, "Hey you, Jim Jim."

The way he yelled it, it sounded a little like Jo Jo or some other Ubangi name and you could see James didn't like the way Mr. Green said it. Because he turns around very fast and drags the bookcase down on the floor with a loud crash.

"Yassa Boss," he said. He would talk this way to Mr. Green sometimes, but I never heard him talk like it to anybody else.

"All right, Jim Jim, pick the damn thing up before you're both down there in the sawdust." Mr. Green could certainly talk tough and the way he had his hand on the hammer made you do the things he asked you to, even James.

James picked up the bookcase and looked over at Mr. Green with a kind of scowl on his face.

"You gonna have that done by a year or two come Christmas," said Mr. Green in the sarcastic way he said things. He said almost everything in a sarcastic way.

"Don matter nohow," James told him. "Ain't got no books to put in it."

Most everybody laughed at that except Mr. Green. "Is that what's been holdin you back," he said, "I suppose you think that the good Lord wouldn't have given you a joint unless you had something like your hand to put in it." I always find that shop teachers and gym teachers bring up sex and things a lot but they're the only men who don't wear ties.

Nobody could figure that out, I still can't, but everybody laughed anyhow, even James, and Mr. Green seemed pretty proud of himself and we noticed he let go of the hammer. James went back to sanding and chiseling the bookcase he didn't have any books to put into and Mr. Green went walking around the room. He came over to my bench where I had this thing I was making. I don't remember what it was now but it had a bottom to it that was supposed to stand up straight and I was sanding these four stubs to make them even. He looked at it and then he looked at me and then he just sort of burst out laughing.

Then he went over to James and said "Jim, Jim, you have got to have pride in your work. Without pride in your work you can never be proud of yourself, you understand." James shook his head, then Mr. Green walked to the front of the class and said, "OK dummies, time to clean up the mess you made out of a days work. Trying to teach you guys carpentry is like making a whorehouse into a church. May the lord help me." Mr. Green was a very religious man and you had to respect him for that.

I really don't think Mr. Green needed the job. I mean he could have made a decent living as a carpenter or a woodworker or something so I think that was why he could say and do the kinds of things he would do.

There was the time when it was raining so hard the streets were getting flooded and everyone knew if it kept up much longer the teachers wouldn't be able to drive home. Cuney High wasn't in the best section of town and most of the teachers lived over on the west side which was quite a distance away and when it rained some of the streets would get so flooded it would cause traffic jams. Anyhow we heard later on that every damn school in the city was dismissed early because of rain, except good old Cuney High.

Mr. Trope the principal would say that if old Roger Cuney, at the age of 65 could hike across mountains in the middle of a snow storm then certainly we could all manage to cross a few puddles. He said this right over the loudspeaker right at a time when we all thought we were going to be dismissed.

Everybody went "aw" and "aw shit" and the room got very noisy and it was very fortunate for some of us who were really mad that we were in Mr. Green's room at the time, because nobody could have gotten any madder than he did. The first thing he did was to get this very red puffed up look on his face and try to imitate Mr. Trope and said something about how Mr. Trope had this rather homosexual thing with the dead Roger Cuney which made it twice as perverted.

Usually Mr. Green would stop us when we were talking too loud but this time he didn't. As a matter of fact what he did do was to turn his back on us for a few minutes and then go sit down in this little office he had off the side of the shop. When he was in this office we would usually get quiet because we knew he went in there to get a shot of this stuff he had in a brown bottle and then he would come out raising hell. This time he poked his head way out and he was grinning just a little bit. He didn't smile much because he had very bad teeth which does not look very good on a teacher. He said, "Jim Jim, take over the class," and then he went back into his little office.

Jim Jim, I mean James got this very surprised look on his face and he looked around at us and we looked at him and then he stood up and walked over to this closet where Mr. Green kept a bunch of these blue aprons and he took one out. He put on the apron while we were all watching him and then he walked to the front bench and said, "All right you dummies, I seed you all fuckin off, now let's get some fuckin pride in your work so you could be proud of yourself." Then he walks over and turns on every damn machine there was in the shop and there was all this shirrin' and buzzing and you couldn't hear yourself think and everybody in the class kind of caught the fever and picked up some wood and started making the funniest things. I mainly remember they were making sexual organs and I was very surprised to see how good they came out although of course they weren't good for anything.

How do you tell a man like Mr. Green that you don't want to be in his curriculum without making industrial arts seem like an inferior curriculum? I thought I would tell him about it when he wasn't so angry but then I got to worrying about it so much that the time never seemed right. And besides Mr. Green was never really not angry except when he was picking on James James. I thought about going back to see Mr. Gallo but that would have been like going behind Mr. Greeen's back, especially when it came to Mr. Gallo, the counselor, because Mr. Green probably hated him worst than Mr. Trope.

It all had to do with Mr. Gallo sending kids like me and all the colored kids to be in Mr. Green's curriculum. When I was working in Mr. Trope's service, I mentioned it to him, that I didn't think that I belonged in the industrial arts curriculum and about the interests and all and he told me to go see Mr. Gallo, but I had already thought about that myself. It all had to do with not wanting Mr. Green to feel inferior so I stayed in the industrial arts curriculum. I realize now that I should have asserted myself except that all those people were so touchy about what they were doing.

I just couldn't get very interested in the shop classes that I had to take but some of the guys were very interesting and the shop teachers would talk dirty because there weren't any girls in the classes. This made you feel more comfortable about being in school and you didn't have to watch out every minute about being neat and using your best English. Some of the guys complained a lot about not having any girls to stare at but Mr. Green said that it wasn't good to have too many distractions. Particularly when you are working with machines that could take a finger off before you missed it.

The one guy in the industrial arts curriculum that I became kind of friendly with was a white guy whose name was Tom Dealy. James James was very amusing but he wasn't easy to have a conversation with. But Tom Dealy was different and he really surprised me because he was having trouble staying in the industrial arts curriculum at the same time I was having trouble getting out. Tom was getting good grades in everything so they had a psychologist come and give him a test too and he told me that he did very high, about 130 which was about 30 points higher than me. Tom was being called in by Mr. Gallo almost every day and Mr. Gallo wanted to put him in the college prep course but Tom didn't want to go into that curriculum. Mr. Gallo arranged that Tom's mother and father and Mr. Trope were all there at one time with Tom and they were all yelling at him about how could he sit by and let all that talent go to waste in the industrial arts curriculum. Tom told me about this a hundred times, that they wouldn't let him be. But Tom was crazy about cars and fixing them and all and he didn't want to go to college but they wouldn't let him alone so after a month of those others screaming about Tom wasting his talent he said he would go into the college prep curriculum.

But when he was with me he was very interested in making and fixing things and used to talk about all the things he might invent. He was a very thin boy, even thinner than James James and he wore these glasses that were very thick and his hair was almost never combed but that wasn't important because it didn't ever interfere

with anything he was doing. Mr. Green didn't say much to Tom
Dealy, I think because he thought Tom was too different from the
others. Tom told me that he went to Mr. Green and asked to help
keep him out of the college prep course. Mr. Green said he would
like to but his hands were tied. That was the only time I ever heard
Mr. Green say his hands were tied.

So one day in homeroom this messenger came from Mr. Gallo's
office with this yellow paper which Mr. Green went over and handed
to Tom. Tom must have known what it was all about because he
picked up his books and stood up and looked right at Mr. Green. Mr.
Green seemed to hunch his shoulders as if to begin to apologize but it
never came out. Then Tom Dealy walked out of the room and never
came back.

After he was gone there was nobody else to talk to unless you
wanted to talk about getting laid and how you managed to get her to
do it. Mr. Green would sometimes listen in on these conversations.
Sometimes I felt he was going too far in trying to be one of the boys
and that he could of had more respect from the guys if he kept his
distance.

Later on, when it looked like I was about to get out of the
industrial arts course again I started thinking about going to college
and becoming something. Then career day came along and I'd like to
tell about that.

Career day was when somebody from almost any kind of job you
can think of comes to the school to tell all about the job and what it
pays and things like that. I went to a couple of them and these guys
really blow their horn for their kind of work, even if you're sure that
it can't possibly be very good. You have to go to at least three rooms
and after your first choice, if you can get in, you usually go to
whatever room is closest.

The year before this one I got to see a carpenter, a mortician, and a
marine who was telling us how great it was to get the marines to
make a man out of you. He was about the worst I saw. Nobody
believed him, except maybe for a guy named Mole, who went up
afterwards and asked him how old you have to be and could you join
even if your mother wouldn't let you.

So I went down this time to hear about being a doctor because I
was still a little interested and had it in the back of my mind, even

though I knew if I got to be one some girl would be after me and her mother too. Anyhow, that's what Mr. Weinberg always told me to make me feel better. But you have to start thinking about some career, especially if it looks like you're going to graduate from high school and have some chance of getting into a college.

Career day reminds me of this guy we called "the Mole" more than anything else and I'll get to why, but first I want to tell a little more about career day.

Career day was one of the principal's big deal things like Roger Cuney's birthday and everyone took it very seriously except the students. Actually, just like the birthday celebration we thought it was kind of a joke and most kids just dropped into rooms to hear people talk about careers that they were most unlikely to go in to.

These people in the community would come down to the school and give us all the crap about how doing what they do would be a great idea. If anybody ever gave a test on what these people said most of the students would flunk it.

One time I dropped in to hear a guy talk about selling cars and that was pretty interesting. Not the guy, but what happened.

When it was time to start the talk there were only four of us in the room and the speaker was still waiting for the group to show up. We knew we were it. Mr. Trope, the principal poked his head in and when he saw how popular this talk was he told the man to hold off because the bell schedule probably confused a lot of the students and they were on their way. He came back about four minutes later with about ten guys and one girl and told them to go sit down. He told the car salesman that they couldn't find the room. One of the guys who got dragged in told me later that they were all about to dig this beautiful lady who was talking on being a beautician when Trope showed up and wouldn't let them get away with it. He called Trope a son of a bitch about three times.

I never found out how the girl got sucked in.

Just about the time that the car salesman started to talk, in walked Flail, the vice-principal. He gave us all a stare as he moved to the back of the room where he stood watching. I guess Mr. Trope wanted to make a good showing for the car salesman by having the V.P. in, but mainly I thought that the principal was afraid that these guys who got dragged away from the beautician might cause trouble.

The car salesman started out by saying how it gave him a great feeling of pleasure to be able to put beautiful pieces of machinery into peoples garages so they could go around with dignity instead of in an old clunker. He said that every time he unloaded a car, then he changed it to sold one, he felt like he was doing his bit to beautify the community.

You wouldn't believe the crap he was handing us. He even brought patriotism into it. He said that every time somebody inked a contract he was doing his bit to hold up the American economy and how patriotic that was.

The last part of the talk was for our benefit, like how it was important to get a good education so you could know how to get along with people and speak good English so you could talk people into buying, and write up sales contracts and stuff like that. He said that you really have to know physiology but I think he meant psychology. He might not have said all those things if Mr. Flail wasn't in the back or if he wasn't in a school.

He also said that you have to be honest with customers about the bad points of a car as well as the good points because a satisfied customer who trusts you always comes back. That's how I got involved because I really didn't believe him about that honesty bit. When he asked for questions I raised my hand. I usually don't do things like that but this time my hand shot up before I thought about it.

I asked him if he thought you should try to sell a car when you really didn't think it was a very good one. I've thought about things like that a lot, especially about all the lousy things people buy. Somebody must sell it to them.

He told me that you should believe in your product and then asked if there were more questions.

I raised my hand again and said "sure, but what if it's no good." Some of the kids laughed but Mr. Flail started coughing hard.

I don't remember what the man answered. I only know that Mr. Flail kept clearing his throat. I do remember the man saying something about how honesty was the best policy and that some people have it in for the businessman and have nothing better to do than go around making up stories about how everybody is always trying to cheat them.

I started to say how some of those people might be right and was about to say why I thought so but Mr. Flail said we were just about out of time and that we should give the man a big hand for his contribution to the education of the community and we clapped a little bit. Mr. Flail went up to talk to the man and we all had to sit and wait around for about 20 minutes until the bell rang.

I decided when I got out of there that I really wasn't very interested in being a car salesman so I was standing in the hall looking for another talk to go to when Mr. Flail came up to me and asked me to wait for him on the bench in his office. I waited through the whole next period but he never showed up till it was over. Then he came in and told me that he was sorry that he had told me to wait because he really didn't want to talk to me after all but if I were interested in career guidance that I should make an appointment to talk with Mr. Gallo. I said I would and I did later.

I met the Mole in the hall afterwards, I think his real name was Clifford something but nobody called him anything but Mole except a couple of teachers. Some other teachers who were friendlier also called him the Mole. Most teachers didn't call on him at all because he stuttered.

He was one of those that got in to hear the talk on being a doctor.

I asked him how it was just to make conversation. Like I said before, we weren't really friendly because of the competition thing we had going in Spanish. He said, "Ve Ve Ve ry gu gu good." I guess it's easier to just tell you what he said because it's very hard to write it the way he talked. It took him a long time to get it out, but he told me that he was interested in being a doctor since he was ten years old when his mother brought him home this book called *A Doctor in the House*. He said his mother made him read it almost every night before he went to bed, and then when he got older she got him a bunch of books about this same doctor who had a lot of interesting adventures. He also said that the only nights he was allowed to stay up late was when there were these TV shows about doctors on. His hero was Dr. Kildare. The Mole was a very honest guy the way he told me all about himself, and we weren't even very friendly. A lot of guys would want to keep some things that he told me secret. I guess I'm pretty easy to talk to though because I ask a lot of questions and am usually very interested in what they have to say. A couple of people have told me that.

He told me he felt very bad about going in front of me in Spanish class but he had to do it because he needed good grades to get into medical school. Our Spanish teacher would move us back and forth on the row with every test we took. I told him I understood.

It's very sad when I think about that little talk the Mole and I had because he never made it to medical school. He didn't even make it through high school because about two or three weeks after that when Mrs. Beeverly called on him to read in Spanish he stuttered so hard that he got Mrs. Beeverly all flustered and she started in on him. She told him that if he didn't stop stuttering she'd never call on him again and he got kind of white and tried it again and stuttered so bad he couldn't even get the first word out so he just sat down and never talked again. I mean it, something happened to him right then and after that nobody could get him to talk a word so they told him if he wouldn't talk then he'd have to go to a special school. I got the story from the nurse a couple of weeks later and she said the Mole was in this hospital and he was just standing around staring out into space and nobody could get through to him. I may have been the last person to have a talk with him.

I heard a couple of people blamed it on Mrs. Beeverly but I don't really think it was all her fault at all. She usually let him talk even though he stuttered except I guess this one day she didn't have as much patience as she usually had.

I remember George once telling me that he had given up trying to get a date with any of the girls in the school until he got out of the vocational arts curriculum. He knew it was a shuck, but he was still victimized by it. The ones he was interested in were not, according to his assessment, about to spend their precious time with somebody who might end up being a carpenter or a drill press operator.

The status shuck, as George portrays it, and as he understood it, centered around the business of what your academic standing had to say about how successful you were likely to be in the future. It all revolved around the forces that were allocating one student to the college campus and another to the shops or the streets. High school is a decisive time. It comes as just about the most difficult of all the developmental stages and it does nothing about the problem except to intensify it by imposing status considerations upon all the others. What it means to be entering adulthood is invidiously converted into a question about one's worth as a potential occupational type.

Females, I have found, are forced to depend on physical qualities in high demand for their potentiality to improve or maintain their status. Regardless of all the shuck questionnaires which contend that such qualities as personality and common interests guide the dating choices of high school students, it's usually the girls with the big eyes and breasts that go out with the class president.

Within the school itself, it is clear that the status of a teacher is reflected by the potential status of the students. This social regularity holds within schools and across schools. Teachers who do their thing in schools where the majority of students go to college have more status than those who teach kids who won't make it to the campus. Within the school, the Mr. Green's of the world don't seem to enjoy much prestige.

With respect to the Mole, what more do we need to say? The drive up the ladder in this society requires too much to allow students (children) to do it all alone. We owe it to them to give them the push up the ladder that they really want, or so we think. Even if we break their backs and minds in the process.

Now if we focus on the system that manages the lives of students, propelling them to compete for status because of the career consequences involved, we begin to see the possibility for change. Status is linked to categories of things like curriculum, grades, honors, physical features, and sometimes skills—as in athletics. One school system in the east tried to combat the structure on its own terms and it worked. What they did was to build a beautiful, million-dollar high school for vocational students only. They advertised it as a dream place to go to school and made students compete to get in. They even refrained from taking as many as they could handle in order to maintain the image that this vocational school had high status. It did uplift the image of the vocational student, but this is not my idea of an ideal alternative. My idea (again refer to Chapter Ten for a more precise description of the structure) is to shift the orientation of the high school from a career structure to one that focuses on learning about self and improving "learning how to learn" skills. Let industry take over all the career business—sorting, training, interesting, apprenticing, guiding, etc.

One of my colleagues has been sleeping with one of his students off and on now for about three months and she still calls him Doctor. He tells her she doesn't have to but she says it doesn't feel right to call him by his first name.

I work out of the School of Education but I teach a course that sociology majors and others take, so I get to meet many students from other fields. I most enjoy the engineering majors who are taking an education elective and suddenly realize they hate what they are doing. One such student came into my office a few weeks back to tell me about his problem. He was tall and lanky and had short hair which I think he was trying to grow long. I'd noticed him in my class from his pained expressions.

He started out by saying that he enjoyed my course and was grateful for the opportunity to think about things and discuss important issues. He told me the field of education was really interesting to him.

"Are you considering switching?" I asked him.

"No, I can't do that," he said with a laugh and a small shrug. "No, that would be impossible." He kept shaking his head long after he gave his answer.

I waited for him to stop being so sure. "Why is that?"

"What?" he said, still thinking about it.

"How come?"

"No, I'm graduating next quarter. And I'm engaged."

"Do you like what you're doing?"

"No, look," he said, "I know you'll understand this but, like you said in class, some of us are just socialized to be a certain way."

"What do you mean?" I asked. I knew what he meant.

"I mean, things just work out a certain way and we really can't have much to say about it."

I just nodded.

"I mean I've come all this way and my parents expect me to finish. They put out a lot to help me get this far."

"Wouldn't they rather see you happy in your work?" I asked naively.

"Yes," he said, "but not as a teacher."

"Why not?"

"It's just not something they think men should be, unless of course (to make me feel better, I suppose) it was to be a college professor."

"Why do you think they feel that way?"

"Well you know how it is. They're from the old country and get all hung up on prestige. They think teaching is for girls."

"What do you think?"

"I suppose I go along somewhat."

"How about your fiancee?"

"What about her?"

"Does she go along too?"

"I don't know for sure," he said, thinking about it. "We've never talked about it. She is in one of the better sororities," he added as an afterthought.

He was obviously troubled about that too. The more we talked, the more things appeared to bother him. I didn't know where to go from there, so I just left it up to him.

"I guess it's all settled then," I said with a slight smile.

"Yea," he answered standing, and more distracted than ever, "I suppose so. Thanks for your time," he said, without looking and turning to go.

"Anytime" I said, "by the way . . ."

He turned again, "Yea?"

"What did you come to see me about?"

I suppose the Greek system of fraternities and sororities is dying out and I honestly believe that this is a good thing. But I think that I'll miss all the good-natured vicious arguments I used to have about them with my students. Nobody seems to want to defend them anymore. I don't really think the issues were trivial and it was useful, particularly in my sociology classes, to make the analogy between them and the status system within the larger society.

One of the more interesting battles we fought concerned the self-aggrandizing use of the school paper by fraternity and sorority members. When some of us were pushing for more political and personal relevance in school journalism, these members still wanted to advertise their social incest. They would take up two or three pages of the newspaper with stuff like:

Miss Joanne Bellows of Kappa Alpha Rho announces her engagement to Mr. Jason Troot of Sigma Beta Pi. The announcement was made by Miss Bellows' mother, Mrs. Robert Bellows of Park Drive, San Marino, at a cocktail party at the Pasadena Hills Hotel attended by five hundred friends of the couple's parents. Mr. Troot's parents, Dr. and Mrs. William Troot of Holby Hills, were present. Miss

Bellows is an elementary education major and plans a teaching career. Mr. Troot has been accepted by the Jefferson Medical College of Philadelphia. The couple plans a June wedding.

After a long struggle we worked out a compromise, where the fraternities and sororities would cut their advertisements for themselves and the elitism they had inherited from their parents and other members to one issue per month. One of my graduate students decided to fight even this as a matter of principle, and made the following announcement in the next issue:

Miss Jane Willows of Beverly Hills announces her forthcoming cohabitation with Henry Clay Brown of Watts. The announcement was made at a party at a friend's house in Venice Beach. The friend wishes to withhold his name from the announcement. Miss Willows' mother was in attendance. Her father, currently estranged from his third wife, was not able to be reached. The couple, both sociology majors, plan either to drop out in the fall and join a commune being organized in Taos, New Mexico, or to go to Canada, depending on Mr. Brown's draft status. No engagement or marriage is planned.

These egocentrisms ended about six months later and were never heard of again, although I understand they are still very much part of the outside culture, which I seldom confront. On the campus, the more invidious remnants of the Greek system appear to be operating within a larger context, and I would suspect one more difficult to comprehend.

In the old days you could easily figure out which frats and which sororities were matching up for mutual self-aggrandizement. The old patterns still continue, but it is difficult to locate the basis of it all. It must be in the informal clique systems that survived the relevancy movement on the campus. The same kind of girls who always ended up with the medical students are still ending up with them. And the same guys who could never get a date with the upper-crust sorority chicks are still having the same problems. The members of the tennis team still date the pom pom girls and the rejects from the sorority system are still majoring in social work. The girls who know a shrimp fork from a frog leg's fork still get asked out to restaurants, and the daughters of teachers and social workers are still sleeping with the intellectuals and eating tacos, and the black girls from the middle classes who straighten their hair still get asked to join the new "relevant" sororities faster than the ones from the ghetto.

I've been on the campus for 15 years now, as student and professor, and I can swear everything is different, but every time I analyze it, it always turns out to be the same.

CHAPTER FIVE

The Professional Shuck

Professional shucking in schools is the special province of the teachers. Students are only relevant to this analysis as we attempt to understand the process of professionalizing, that is, how we make professionals out of nonprofessionals.

Teachers, for the most part, do consider themselves professionals. This is meant usually to contrast with blue-collar workers, who do such unprofessional things as join labor unions and go out on strike. Being a professional involves other considerations too, things teachers *do* rather than the things they don't do. A professional teacher is one who holds his or her position, or status, or power, or security, by virtue of holding (usually) a college degree and a credential.

Another quality of professionalism in teachers is the attainment of an intellectual, rather than a manual, skill. Most teachers believe that what they do well (a) cannot be done by anyone else without proper training, and (b) is expressed in their everyday performance, even though they cannot put it into words.

Some others of us believe that (a) any half intelligent adult or adolescent, without any training at all, can do as well in short order, and (b) the reason most teachers cannot articulate the scope and depth of their unique intellectual skill is that there is no such thing.

Professionalism is also manifested by dressing better than nonprofessionals. In the absence of performance, there is always coat and tie and whatever it is that professional ladies wear, bought, preferably on a charge account at any of the better local status stores. Furthermore, professionalism is a matter of keeping up with the knowledge and skills of the profession, much like doctors reading the AMA and other medical journals. Now then, I invite you to look over the reading room of an average school and see how teachers keep up. In my old school, we had mainly such women's magazines as the *Ladies Home Journal* and *Harper's Bazaar,* and in the men's smoking room we had *Playboy* and a bunch of magazines about cars. I've been around to a lot of teachers' rooms in the past ten years and I believe I am correct when I say that, as far as what is available in the schools, teachers mostly keep up with what is popularly being driven and worn and crocheted and bought, in the society at large.

But this isn't quite fair. Strictly speaking, in order to keep up professionally there has to be something to keep up with, and that's another shuck having to do with what goes on in the super profession of higher education, which I'll discuss later. The real shuck of professionalism involves the maintenance of the claim that teachers deserve authority because they are professionals, not because they can do anything.

A senior Harvard psychologist once related a story of the time he was invited to participate in drawing up criteria for licensing professional psychologists in the state of Massachusetts. His suggestion to the committee was that if the candidate for licensing could prove he could help somebody, he would receive a license, but if he couldn't, he would be granted a Ph.D.

Teachers who take my summer courses usually do so to obtain credits to get either increases in salary or a raise in position or status, or to expand their "social horizons," that is, find spouses. I have often asked them to describe what it is they do that nonprofessionals can't do. They usually insist, after much stumbling, that it's all intuitive. If so, I have always wondered, why would an intuitive housewife not be able to do just as well? But that sounds sexist, which it is, and gets us into another important dimension of the professionalism shuck. I have no doubt that our society is sexist to the core. This is expressed in many forms of occupational discrimination, but is founded upon the entirely unrelated assumption that women best take care of children, while men best take care of income and social status. I am personally bitter about this because I am a teacher-educator, and this often turns out to mean that I train young women to become teachers so they can support their fiances or husbands through graduate, law, or medical school. This indirectly means I am supporting the law profession and the medical profession. Put another way, law and medical professors neither support me nor do their graduates see themselves as simply the instruments of the professional advancement of someone else.

I don't want to overstate the case. Some young women are committed, and many women come back for teacher training after their own children are in school. There are many varieties of female involvement in education, and some of them are not dependent on whatever it is they are trying to do with their lives in reaction to a man. But from where I stand, the overwhelming impression is that the majority of the women with whom I work—and I work mainly with women, because men need more money and prestige than teaching offers—are in it for less than what I might call professional reasons.

The first university class I taught took place in one of those large, terraced classrooms. The course title was "Foundations of Education," and it was a requirement for teachers. I was told to expect an enrollment of over a hundred. Being appropriately nervous, I don't remember exactly how I made it across the room to my place behind a wooden lectern. I felt as if I were in a vise. I arranged my well-typed lecture notes in front of me, took a deep breath, and looked up, and up, and up. One hundred and fifty females were looking down at me, right at me, expecting something.

Without hesitation, I went right into my own professional shuck. It controls the anxieties. Toward the end of that first class, feeling more comfortable, I gave my well-prepared lecture on the education profession. I talked mainly about women in education. Remember now, I was the only male in the room, and I said something about why women go into education. I talked about the surveys of reasons they say they do it, because they love children and want to help them learn and grow and develop, and other good things. I claimed even then, as I do now, that this is and was bullshit.

Women really go into education, I said, because (a) it's an easy curriculum, (b) they're accepted into the field, (c) they have to study something in college since the only other alternatives are secretarial and clerical work and they'd rather be in the university than doing those jobs, (d) it provides a nice income while single and a good income supplement when married, (e) they've had the good, moralistic training we require of teachers, (f) as long as they only plan to work a couple of years, they wouldn't want to invest too much time in preparation (as in law, engineering, or medicine), (g) it gives them security after raising children, (h) it gives them holidays and summers off to be with their own children or for travel, or (i) they are highly committed to professional education.

The girls looked at me from on high with bewilderment, disgust, and most with total disinterest. For better than half the class members, I was only making a point they figured they'd better note down in case I asked a question about it on the final exam. I might just as well have said that better than 50 percent of all college girls were nymphomaniacs—they would have mindlessly copied it down. From that point on, my anxieties were reduced. If your students are disinterested, they aren't about to challenge you. Then I went on to talk about why women stay in education. Who is it that is there in the classroom?

I said something about the large contingent of women who come back after their youngest child is in the first grade. On the average (2.5 children an average of 2.8 years apart), these women have missed from 10 to 14 years. Many of them don't even take a refresher course, since they have kept up their credentials and that's all one needs to be a professional teacher. These women, as we might expect, rank their role preference in this order: first, mother; second, wife; third, teacher. The meaning of this for professionalism I leave to your conjecture.

A second large group, to whom I have already alluded, are the "trousseau twoers," who are getting ready for marriage, or the "supporters" who are getting their husbands ready for fortune. I don't know how large this group is anymore, but I did check on a survey at my own school and found that three years after graduation better than 70 percent of our girls were not in the classroom.

A third group are those that were hoping marriage would take them away from all this, but it never happened. Some of these have made a decent adjustment, but many haven't.

A fourth group, though small in size, is significant because of their longevity. These are the lesbians who have no interest in marriage or babies. They may be among our most committed teachers, but I know it would be outrageous, considering the state of sexual liberation in our culture, to recommend that school boards seek them out and offer them jobs.

Finally, God bless them, are those who really care about the quality of education children get (this does not exclude members of the latter group), and put themselves out to make it possible. If I were to venture a guess as to their numbers I would put this estimate at less than 10 percent of the total. Some of them may also have their mother and their wife roles, but they, unlike the others, consider their professional identity as significant as do their men.

This was the content of my first lecture. And, without my knowledge, a senior professor of some scientific subject was listening from behind the door to my rather abrasive comments on the teaching profession. The following morning my dean called me in and advised me I was overheard to have said all teachers were either old maids or lesbians. Later I discovered that the senior professor who blew the whistle on me had a wife who was a teacher.

Needless to say, I survived both the first lecture and the senior professor's tattling. I still talk about the same subject but now I am careful to emphasize the good women in teaching so each student will think I am talking about her. Also, I invite the people standing outside into my classroom.

In our teacher-training programs we emphasize the behavioral sciences. This orientation is a pure shuck, for the major use of the behavioral sciences in teaching is to upgrade the sophistication of the future teacher without improving his or her ability to do anything in the classroom. The teacher can describe a rat experiment utilizing princi-ples of reinforcement, but can find very little use for it in the classroom. The teacher can use such shuck words as "regression," "fixation," "socialization," "family disorganization," and even "culturally disadvantaged,'' without having the faintest idea of how the concepts can or cannot be related to the behavior of children.

Psychology has given us a large share of our training knowledge, especially the test. The good old standardized test, especially the IQ test, has come to be one of the worst shucks ever perpetrated upon school children. I would have little objection to the existence of the test, despite its cultural bias (white middle-class kids always come out better on tests) and its absurd assumption that a score (99) is a concept (intelligence) and therefore is a reality (indicating our innate ability to think), if it weren't for the fact that teachers and administrators make use of them. I agree with those who say this is happening less and less, but, unfortunately, the IQ test will continue to wreck the lives of human beings long after it has ceased to exist. The test may be discarded, but the notion of testing which the IQ test made both respectable and necessary will hang on for decades.

One shuck inherent in testing is the way in which it manufactures an occupation for test makers and test teachers, a basis of decision-making for educators, and a waste of time for kids. Take, for example, the interest test.

The way we professionalize any educational task is to administer these scientific instruments, called occupational interest inventories, to make scientific predictions about what we would really be happy doing. So a kid walks into the counselor's office, and he comes out with a score on a test. This is supposed to tell him how he should spend the rest of his life. He then gets placed in school programs according to this score and other scores like IQ and grade averages, and he is already programmed to go in a certain direction at 12 or 15 years of age.

Unfortunately, we also have scientific information telling us that about 80 percent of our population is unhappy in their work. It seems to me we either need a better interest test or a way of finding out who a person is that uses less science and a little more humanity.

Talking about tests reminds me of a conversation with George right after he had been professionally sorted out into the vocational curriculum. He came into my office feeling very low and had some trouble raising his eyes or his head. I asked him what had happened, and he told me. He said that he had taken all these tests and the counselor was sending him to industrial arts.

"What do you mean?" I asked him. "That's not for you."

"Well, I don't know," he said, "I saw the scores."

"Do you believe them?" I asked.

"Well," he said, after a thoughtful moment, "I don't see why tests would lie."

I felt as if I just had eaten about a dozen rotten eggs: I knew George was feeling bad because he believed he had just learned something very disappointing about himself, not just because he was being sent into the shops where he didn't want to be.

"George," I said, "tests aren't mind readers. There can be mistakes."

"That's what I thought, and I told the counselor, but she told me she was getting her license as a school psychologist so she knew about things like that and I didn't."

I nodded my head. That's a tough combination to beat: a test and a psychologist. It took us a year to straighten out this particular problem for George.

The alternative to maintaining those structures which professionalize education would require that we:

1. Redefine what a teacher is to allow for persons who have not come through the credentialing process to try their hand at it. By redefinition I am only asking that we no longer assume that a teacher is, by definition, a person with a teaching credential. After all, most of us would agree that Socrates was a teacher even though he couldn't get a job in our public schools.

2. Find a way to defeminize teaching, to create a sexual balance. The old consciousness way of doing this would be to pay more money, require higher degrees, and become male chauvinistic about who gets in, but that's the old game. The new game would have to be one that would require the kinds of extensive commitments that would deter income-supplementing housewives to see teaching as an easy "other role."

3. Take teacher training out of the university where it gets mixed in as one of the many alternative curricular choices for college students. When it is not an alternative to law or medicine or engineering it cannot be inferior, can it? This suggestion is only a part of my earlier suggestion to eliminate career concerns from formal education.

4. Eliminate testing from the educational enterprise entirely, thereby making irrelevant the professionalization of those who understand testing. Better to begin with no skills than with those that are detrimental, even though they confer a "professional" status. Many may think that testing is a trivial example but in an insidious way the idea of the test (some kind of test) has come to form the backbone of professionalism in education. People who make up tests or use them, mostly psychologists and those who have been brainwashed by them, have come to believe that an expert, or professional, is one who can construct a test for any purpose, or create a purpose for any test. Tests are used as measures of some state of educational existence in the business called research; and research is the name of the professional "game" at the higher levels of educational functioning. This gets us into the scientific shuck, which combines nicely with the idea of professionalism.

The professional expert in education is the person who most approximates the scientist. He has the capacity to convert all reality into numbers and numbers into all reality. By using all of these numbers he comes up with something referred to as "truth." A typical educational scientific truth might be one that holds that method A is superior to method B. Now we come to know this truth by comparing scores of students exposed to method A with those exposed to method B. If the difference between them is numerically large enough, given a few other scientific inputs, we can conclude truth.

The assumptions upon which our scientific professionals operate are numerous. The following are a few of them:

1. Human beings are appropriate subjects for scientific inquiry
2. Our observations mean what we say they mean
3. Observations can legitimately be converted into numbers
4. Abstractions like learning can be represented by anything we choose; for example by a score on a test.
5. As a scientist I see what I say I see

The colossal shuck behind educational scientism is that for years its practitioners have gotten away with their claim that education is an appropriate field of scientific exploration. This is analogous to Catholic missionaries in Latin America who claim that all Latin Americans are Catholic simply because the Catholic Church has established itself everywhere. So too have the educational scientists colonized us. Everything a professor of education does unless he was fortunate enough to have gotten his background in philosophy, extends the scientific-expert-professional stranglehold these true believers have on us. We get promoted according to the number of scientific articles we publish, and we publish only scientific articles (unless we can't do statistics) because that's mainly what our professional journals will publish.

A short time back a good friend of mine did a study which analyzed the procedures of a scientific journal. He looked at the criteria by which the journal rejected submitted articles. It turned out the criteria were invoked only intuitively, when they were used at all. At times scientist reviewers were observed to have sent letters which supported both an acceptance and a rejection, depending on what the editor wanted to do. On other occasions, bad science by a well-known man in the field was accepted over good science by an unknown—in other words, the same old status shuck.

We've all read that statistics can make anything come out the way you want it to; since it has to come out positive to be published, what can you expect? People in the business hear a lot about how a researcher manufactures data to make things come out his way, but I understand that it really isn't necessary, since you can always make something out of nothing if you're good with numbers.

The most frightening thing about this shuck is the way the numbers have us by the balls.* Most pros now have their computer games going for them and once realities get translated into concepts, and concepts get divided into (usually arbitrary) classes or categories, and these categories get assigned numbers and the pros start playing with the numbers, what happens to the reality with which we started? There's no way to make IBM cards bleed, so how do we remind the scientists they started with people?

But we do start with people, and that often turns out to be a shuck too. When I worked on my first study I was really convinced I was into science. I was working on a 30-page questionnaire, and I was supposed to get answers from a bunch of illiterate juvenile delinquents who were being forced by the school principal to answer all my questions on threat of expulsion or worse.

---

*A sexist remark, but appropriate to higher professionals as a rule.

The interviews went something like this. I walked the kid from his classroom down to a little room they had given for interviewing, which was next to the vice-principal's office. The boys were about 15 and black; I was 25 and white. They were poor, and I was middle class. I never broke a law in my life; hardly a day went by when they didn't break at least one. I sat behind a desk with a big notebook and they sat on a chair which I'm sure they recognized was from the vice-principal's office. Now we were here, ready to get into scientific work.

I had been trained for a week at the government's expense to do this interview. Most of the science projects I worked on were at the government's expense.

Anyhow, I got into my questions. "How many members in your family?"

"Changes from day to day," he told me. It sounded like he was trying to be helpful.

I didn't have that category on my check sheet, so I tried again. "Well, when you're all together, how many are there?"

"Ain't never together."

I went on. "How many schools have you attended?"

"Don't know," he said, "some I attended, some I didn't."

"I mean, enrolled at."

"A bunch, maybe seven or nine."

I checked eight. "OK, now, I want you to try to remember the first time you ever got into trouble in school. Do you remember when that was?"

"First day, probably."

"Don't you remember?"

"Seems like I always been in trouble, way back."

I checked "early." I asked him about his friends and he told me he had some but they changed a lot so I was unclear about that also.

After about 15 minutes of similar difficulties, we got into the core of the study, his aspirations and perception of his opportunities.

"What would you like to do in the future?" I asked.

"When?"

"Oh, like next year or the year after that."

"Oh," he said, as if he had just figured it out, "when I gets outa here maybe I'll try some college. You know something about that," he said. "You think it's a good idea to go to college?"

"Oh, I don't know," I said, "you know, college isn't for everybody."

He knew a shuck when he heard one. "Oh, you think it's not for me."

"I didn't say that," I defended, but I think I did.

"Oh," he said, letting me off.

"Tell me," I went on, knowing that I was trapped by my commitment to hand in a completed interview, "do you think you'll have any trouble getting into college?"

"Sheet, man," he said, stretching his body along the lines of the chair, "you know well as I do that there's got to be trouble."

Good, I thought, now I'm getting something worth turning in. "Where's the trouble as you see it?"

"That's the trouble, man."

"What?"

"I don't see it."

"See what?"

"The trouble."

I wrote it down. It was as meaningless as the rest of my data. When I finished I walked him back to his classroom and asked him to send out the next kid on the list. The smile they gave each other convinced me I was wasting my time.

I've found interviewing to be a failure time and time again. I can write down the words but I really don't know what they mean. I suppose it's important to continue working on a science of man's behavior, but as far as education is concerned, nobody seems to be doing much to improve what's going on in the classroom, even though the government has poured many millions of dollars into this professional work.

The government spent about two million dollars on the study I have described. I tried to track it down, years later, to see what happened to it. I found a monograph over in the library and a couple of published articles that had helped the director get promoted, but nothing that ever helped any delinquent kids adjust to school. I do remember the original proposal for the money had lots of uses for the findings but I found out much later that that was also just a shuck. Nobody really expects anybody to do anything with what they find out. They just think it's something one ought to say as long as we're draining the public's money. As scientists, of course, we are not expected to do anything with our findings. Scientists just discover truth and lowerlings make whatever use of it they can; that is, unless there's profit to be made out of it. In my department alone, there are at least a half dozen scientists who have translated their scientific work into flourishing consulting firms, often selling a variation of products or skills that accrued out of studies supported by the government.

So the harsh point to be made here is that millions of dollars from governmental agencies and foundations are poured into the professional shuck. My personal evaluation is that about 98 percent of the money goes into helping the professionals maintain or improve their status; supporting graduate students through school; uplifting the status of the school or university that brings in the grant; increasing the amount of data in our scientific pools; and keeping the computers running, which supports programmers, key-punch operators, and scientists, who get their kicks figuring out new, cute things for the big machines to do. The other 2 percent of the money may go into helping kids learn, but I doubt it.

A case in point is the university Research and Development Center. These new organizations of educational professionals take a considerable bite out of the money available for studying education. There are a bunch of them throughout the country, and my guess is that they are all pretty much the same, except for the topic each has chosen for study. The R and D center as a way of life, points out what can happen to the campus environment when the professionals and ''scientists'' get a foothold.

The first thing that happens is that the college or school in which the center is located starts looking a bit more like a corporate bureaucracy, education's answer to ETS, or a Madison Avenue advertising agency. They hire a couple of administrators who have the bureaucratic personality, people who excel at meetings and making out budgets, high task-low affect types; then they recruit from their own faculty and elsewhere a bunch of people who make tests, and they're in business. The R and D centers keep up the respectability of the school both in appearance and productivity. They try not to get involved in campus affairs, since students are basically irrelevant except as a cheap labor pool. If they can manage it they manipulate the budget to include wall-to-wall carpeting and executive office furniture. Eventually they succeed in looking nothing like a campus activity, unless we can now argue that their image of what a college should be is more the trend today.

My major objection is that these caricatures of professionalism perpetuate, even expand upon, the notion that research and development in education is simply an extension of what psychologists do or want done. In our center there are a bunch of people involved in exactly what they would be involved in if they worked in a test construction factory. Fortunes are spent making up tests. And why do these people make up tests? Because the psychologists who dominate the decisions of the center are good at making up tests. The topic of study for the center is evaluation. How can we study evaluation? One way is to make up tests that evaluate. If the topic were interpersonal relations, they'd make up tests for that. It turns out, and I'm sure the same is true for other centers, that whatever the people do best is what the problem calls for. It reminds me of a study of mental institutions I read recently, where the majority of the patients happened to have the kind of problems in which the psychiatrists specialized.

By evaluation, the professionals in the center mean a process that they have invented to either evaluate or help others evaluate. It isn't all testing but it is the business of creating an experience in your own image. Our evaluation pros get hold of school leaders and show them how to evaluate, assess the needs of schools, or whatever. They have a model for doing this and by getting people to act in terms of this model they begin to create an environment rather than to assess one.

"Needs assessment" is a good shuck term which these professionals use a lot. It just turns out to be a perpetuation strategy in which needs are whatever fits the model and the skills of the professionals to supply. In most schools, in my experience, needs jump up at you like a jack in the box. They only become real needs, however, if administrators "discover" them, and if they can be accommodated within the conventional routines of the system. As I see it the biggest need in education is for a little humanity but this is seldom evaluated because no one has the understanding or freedom to do anything about it. A new biology lab, well that's a need that can be met.

The whole business about needs and their assessment is mostly wrapped up in the wedding of politics and finance. Anyone who thinks a need of a Mexican-American reading program has the same evaluative weight as the needs of a bigger and better science program in the city schools is a dreamer. Our pros are not dreamers; professionals seldom are. They make their contribution to schooling only to the extent that "reality" (that is, politics and finance) permits, and it doesn't permit much.

One of the more pertinent events in the R and D shuck story occurs when the superprofessional scientists come to evaluate the progress of the professionals. Just when we start to hear rumors that, in the absence of much to show for so many millions of dollars they've given us, they are going to close down the center, we get a report that more money is forthcoming. My conclusion is either that somebody has convinced the superpros that we are doing something worthwhile, or the superpros have exactly the same vision of the world as our pros. Either way, the feedbag gets filled again.

I think these centers simply illustrate the central issue in the professional shuck: Professionals define themselves by a combination of style and task, and the mutual acceptance of each other's belief systems as to what education should be, never dealing with the issue of what it might be if they hadn't gotten their degrees as psychologists.*

Part of the scientific-professional shuck has its roots in the faith Americans have in scientism. This had led to the emergence of "expertise" in almost every field of study, and, consistent with our core value, expertism, like everything else, is convertible into money.

As I have suggested earlier, our educational professionals are heavily into money. As I look around my school and a few others I quickly detect a strong relationship between scientism and the sudden emergence of private consulting firms. Wisdom is never for sale, but hack scientism is always available at a price. To me this means that educational institutions will pay through the nose for gimmicks that make their reports to superintendents or boards of education look technical, therefore scientific, therefore reliable. But they won't spend a penny for an idea about how to save the schools, or the children, from the disastrous future they face.

I have heard that college campuses years ago were places where dialogues between wise men about ideas could and would take place,

---

*Those who have been trained as anything else seem to be as persuaded (if they thought about it) as the test men that testing and evaluation are almost synonomous. But that is simply another indication of the pervasive impact psychological thinking has had upon all branches of education.

even in such applied studies as education. If one overhears a conversation nowadays, it is most likely to be about the stock market rather than about learning. There seems to be little hope of ever restoring educational studies to the level of an intellectual dialogue, and this I think is because we have become far more obsessed with our status as professional scientists and with economic stability than we are about knowledge.

One last point about the scientific part of the professional shuck. The educator-scientist is usually a man who ignores the subjects of his studies, except, of course, as they become his subjects, their environment his laboratory. He seldom spends time with school children, except to observe them as they complete his scientific tasks. And after many years of this kind of disinterest in children in general and ignorance of them as whole human beings, he reaches the pinnacle of his profession. He becomes an expert in the education of children. It's a bit like becoming an expert in sexual behavior (as some scientists do) without ever going to bed with a member of the opposite sex. The knowledge may very well be valid within the conventions of scientism, but in terms of humanity, I would prefer the experts to be human beings, particularly if they propose to tell me something about how I should conduct a classroom.

Paul Goodman, the once-controversial educator-psychologist-intellectual, has suggested that one of the worst things which ever befell schooling was that a time came when someone felt schools should be administered. Like so many other disasters that befall all of us in our time, we often lose sight of our purpose in the interest of accomplishing the very task which destroys us. We begin fighting for peace and become obsessed with war. We create militarists to defend us and militarists create a world in their own image. We begin working to live and end up living to work.

Trope, my old school principal, used to say "schools would be such pleasant places to work if it weren't for the damn kids." I remember the first time I went for an interview at Cuney High School. At the time I didn't know Trope from Adam, and had no reports on his reputation. I was new in town.

Trope liked my style; I had lots of education, was professionally dressed, and spoke well, and I knew after half an hour I had the job. He asked me if I wanted to look over the campus, and I said I did. He then walked me about two miles around the place, never talking about anything but himself and how everything related to him.

We went to the shop where the students were building boats. "I like the sea," he told me, "and I felt we should conduct the classes in shop around a theme. Have kids work on something they can feel good about." I didn't know at the time that practically none of the kids in the school had ever been on a boat. Boats were about as much a part of their concerns as the deliberations over the Indo-China border.

"I run a tight ship," he told me, "kids need a clear vision of their controls. It provides them with security." I mumbled something that would neither approve nor disapprove.

"I fought this swatting battle through on the Hill time and time again." I have since learned that all field administrators refer to the home office people as "the Hill."

"As long as the teacher keeps his jacket and tie on, the kids know that they are not being hit in anger," he said, raising his arm into swat position. This was one of my first indications that Trope had a different way of viewing the world. I asked for the explanation. Trope was pointing out the major swatting area at this moment.

"We do it out there in case they want to scream. We let them go ahead and do that. Besides, the gym teachers are close by in case the kids decide to fight back." He smiled, as if he remembered an instance.

I asked about the jacket and tie. "That doesn't apply to P.E. teachers," he said, "but still, they are required to dress appropriately at other times."

"No," I said, "I mean the idea of keeping on your jacket while swatting." "Yes, good idea," he said, "lets the kids know that swatting doesn't mean a teacher is losing his dignity."

I thought about it and it made some sense in a bizarre way. It occurred to me I was more interested in questioning the jacket and tie than the business about swatting. By then we were walking along the fence on the far side of the playground. Trope was busily engaged checking out the fence for holes. "We may not want them," he said, joking, "but we have to keep them here the best we can."

As we walked across the yard he asked me where I lived. I told him on the west side of town. He told me he did too. He obviously approved. "We certainly wouldn't want the kids to see us on the street in our old clothes or digging in the garden."

"No?" I asked.

"I've been a principal for a long time now and the one thing I have found to be a guiding principle is that we shouldn't get close to our students. That leads to all sorts of things."

"Like what do you have in mind?" I questioned cautiously.

"Well, like asking for favors," he said, and stopped walking, as if he was clearly convincing.

Later, we walked down the main corridor toward the administrative offices. "I like to keep all the administrators close by," he said. "It's more efficient." I noticed the counselor's office was next to the vice-principal, and asked Trope if he thought of the counselor as an administrator. It was my first experience in a public high school, and I was trying to get some sense of how persons were defined.

"Oh yes indeed," he answered. "They keep the show running. I can call on them for anything from placing students in and out of classes to observing the swat period. They also talk to the kids the teachers can't handle and they either get them to shape up or find another school."

"Do kids mind being sent to the counselor's office?" I asked, naively.

"Of course not, they're there to help them."

I wondered about how the kids would feel being next to the vice-principal's office and two offices down from Trope. Whose side would they think the counselor was on? Later I found out Trope was right; he could count on the counselors for anything. I'm not suggesting for a moment that school counselors should work against administrators, unless of course that means working for the kids.

Trope then got into defining the role of the teacher for me. This was my first experience with professional socialization down on the field of play. I was now to learn what was expected of a teacher, or rather, what Trope expected. I had already gotten a few pointers about not being friendly, holding the line, and running a tight ship.

"Some teachers try to be lenient and a friend to the kids. You new ones always give it a try, and I expect you will too, but you might as well save your time and learn from experience. Give them an inch and they'll take a mile."

I gave another noncommittal "mmmmm."

"A few kids can be trusted to take responsibility and I believe they should have it, but always be sure it's one of our better people. We have a student government and those boys and girls are pretty reliable. We screen them pretty hard, and Mr. Flail, the vice-principal, sits in on all the meetings to make sure nobody decides to make any trouble."

I could see that he'd thought about it.

"Now, Mr. Weinberg, there are a few expectations I have for my teachers and you should know what they are before you decide to accept the job."

By now we were in his office and he was sitting across from me behind his large desk with the picture of the ugly Roger Cuney behind him. I nodded for him to proceed.

"First and foremost, I expect my teachers to be professional men and women. To me that means we dress like professionals, talk like professionals, and act like professionals."

I nodded.

"Yes, indeed," he said. "At all times you must remember who you are and what you represent."

I wasn't about to ask him who I was and what I represented. "Secondly, I expect that my teachers will run a dignified classroom. That means all students sitting quietly at their desks, working. A busy student is a student who is learning something."

I nodded again.

"Thirdly, I expect new teachers to get to know the old ones, to talk to them, to sit in on their classes during your free period or lunch period. There is still no substitute for experience, no matter what all of those leftist college professors tell you. You've got to get that idealism nonsense out of your head. That kind of fuzzy thinking won't hold here in the classroom. It just doesn't work. The teachers I want you to watch, you'll get a list, are those who haven't been in college for 20 years. They've given up all that fuzzy thinking years ago."

"Well, some of them are down to earth," I said, defending the campus, which seemed neutral enough.

"Yes, well, you get my point."

I nodded.

"Finally, at least for now, I expect teachers to be loyal to me, to the Board of Education, to the other administrators, to the department chairmen and their curriculum guides. I, on the other hand, will be loyal in return, and will stand up for a teacher against parents and students, but only if they have acted in line with my expectations.''

Well, I got the job. I found out later that the competition wasn't so rough. Nobody who knew about Trope applied for the job. I also found out that Trope never stood up for his teachers, but that's another story.

For the most part, school administrators, for reasons we can all understand, really believe the school exists for them to run rather than the other way around. Although most will talk about the needs of children, it is still a matter of their decision about what children need, rather than children having the right to create a structure to accommodate their own needs. A professional school man is an organization man, which means that he has learned how to run things. He also believes one does things one has learned to be expedient, and makes the organization over to be consistent with that learning. In fact he acts much the same way as the people who learned about testing.

My experience with Frederich Trope and about five others who were less obvious than he, has convinced me that professionalism, as it relates to school administrators, is a shuck in the sense that while we talk about ourselves as serving the educational needs of children, we are really concerned about maintaining our professional roles and the organization in a state of equilibrium. To talk about all the things we do to kids like herding, swatting, silencing, drilling, grading, detentioning, disciplining, etc., as meeting their needs, is like talking about burning a witch as a way of saving her soul. For some reason, however, when one couches all these atrocities against children under organizational slogans such as ''running a tight ship'' or ''doing an efficient job,'' it doesn't seem quite so evil. And this is why it continues.

School administration has evolved into a professional identity, but I believe it was built upon the latter-day conception of the role rather than the way the role was first conceived. In Chapter Ten I describe the formal organization of the school as a bureaucracy, a hierarchy of positions of control and authority. Unfortunately, the professionalism game has become a mobility game—the more professional one is, the higher one goes and vice versa. The fact that school administrators are usually men, even though most teachers are women, speaks to my point. Most women just don't have the time to be that professional, nor do they have the motivation, knowing how the cards are stacked against them.

The alternative to this vicious system would be the way it probably all started, in a community of equals. Some group of people at some time in the past probably decided that things would get done better if they divided up the jobs, and one person was probably assigned the responsibility for coordinating the whole business. Because this was probably the most difficult task, I wouldn't be surprised if the task didn't circulate among the members of the group. And so it could and should be, with all of the status and superiority-inferiority dimensions eliminated. Many of the new schools operate on this model and it works fine for them. I doubt if the present structure will erode very quickly. It will probably be the last to go. The captain will be the last to leave his sinking ship, because with the ship goes his role and without his role who is he? Only another person.

I have no bone to pick with professionalism when it means control over your life within the organization or when it means keeping your life uncluttered by the absurd demands of the ignorant on how you should conduct your affairs. But it seldom means that. In educational professionalism we have gone in all the wrong directions.

We have gone the route of using status rather than competence to gain respect. We have gone the way of converting schools into efficiency systems because that shows off our technical skills. We have sent students down roads they would not have chosen for themselves, and we have seen them as shadows of their total human potential. We do not talk to them, we test them. We silence their opinions and advice and wisdom with our hierarchies and punishment systems and rules. We have gone the scientific road rather than the human one. These two turn out to be incompatible, not in theory, but in practice. The time has come when we take children to the stars and beyond and praise ourselves for our ability to do so, never considering for a moment that all those poor kids wanted to do was to go across the street, where their spirits lay waiting for them.

CHAPTER SIX

The Allocation Shuck

"Allocation" is a shuck word, at least as it is used by most educators. It is a word borrowed from industry, the same place from which we get our consciousness of reality in the schools. In the "real" world, it refers to a process of organizing and ear-marking resources for specific uses or consumption, and is directly linked to the efficient management of commercial-industrial activities.

In the schools, allocation refers to an efficient way of differentiating students so that all adult occupational roles, from space scientist to broom pusher will be adequately manned. In the secondary schools the allocation structure takes on the form of curriculum. As curricula differ, the hopes and aspirations of students differ. And so do the results.

Some children become lawyers and engineers, some become sewer cleaners, some will go to prison for a good portion of their lives. The curriculum a student takes in high school is an excellent predictor of which path he is likely to follow after graduation. We may not be able to discern which students will become prisoners, but we can generally predict which ones won't. These are the ones who will not need to chance it, because the things people go to prison for are readily available in the legal way.

The allocation shuck really begins much earlier, and involves a number of separate processes we think of as every day kinds of schooling. It involves certain assumptions about children so basic that most educators would consider it outrageous even to question them.

There is the assumption, for example, that children have different interests from one another. And there is the idea that males and females are different from each other in the kind of work they can or should do. Also, there is the assumption that clean students are better able to hold professional jobs than messy ones. Another assumption is that of differing intelligence. This one breaks down into subassumptions such as (a) we can really measure intelligence, (b) we can relate it to types of work, and (c) high intelligence should lead to the kind of work that brings the highest social rewards. Then there are the assumptions that bright kids deserve better teachers, and that rich kids shouldn't even *want* to be auto mechanics.

Later on in schooling we evolve a new set of assumptions, such as, girls with sexy bodies can't possibly conceive of becoming lawyers or scientists. And in our most lucid moments we can't begin to fathom how a kid who can't control his emotions or sexual needs can possibly expect to be a college professor.

Perhaps some clarification is needed. *Children have different interests.* Now, that is a neutral, somewhat unimaginative assumption. Why should it be challenged? Where does it go? Well, we assume that interests reflect something biological and are relatively permanent. Nonsense! It is likely that all children, experience and encouragement being equal, are capable of becoming interested in all things, at one time or another. And yet, with what we call our objective perspective, we reach out with pincerlike claws and in a moment of a child's life, encapsulate him, set up his life for him as rigidly as a steel tunnel. Of course we shuck this away on the grounds that we are thus providing children with outlets to their unique interests.

A friend of mine, now a dropout on a beach somewhere in the southland, loves to tell the story of how he became an engineer. For the first 10 years of his life his major preoccupation was sky staring and a little poetry. At the age of 11, some uncle gave him a tinker toy and he became very involved with it. He started building a castle in the sky, which his psychiatrist, years later, interpreted as his desire to climb up and disappear. His parents, who seemed to have been waiting 11 years for some interest to appear in their child, latched onto this activity as if it were a sign that his calling were being determined from above or beyond. His dad went out and bought him a metal tinker toy set large enough to be shaped into life-sized buildings. The kid was caught in the expensive purchase. Being well socialized, he knew better than to tell his parents he wasn't particularly interested or appreciative, so he went dutifully to work and ground out some atrocity of a bridge that connected to his wooden castle. Well, one thing led to another and before he knew it he was enrolled in a school of engineering for a five-year jaunt.

Now he insists that he protested his fate, time and again, and assures all that his parents were neither callous nor brutal. They gave him every opportunity to come up with an alternative. The only thing they insisted upon was that he had to take something in college because he had to go. The alternative to that was uncertain. When you feel trapped by the demand to communicate some identity (interest), the human way is choosing something, anything, rather than be faced with no social role whatever.

Everybody agreed that the tinker toy caper was significant, and this led to the school of engineering. Five years later, and caught up in the shuck that "one is supposed to finish what one starts," he graduated from the college of engineering in the middle of his class. When it came time to get a job he made another mistake of consciousness. He assumed that since he was qualified to work as an engineer he should do so. And so he did, for 15 years. He was totally bored the entire time, but didn't suspect there was anything wrong in that, since he was getting a good salary and had nice vacations. What more could one expect?

Then came the anxieties and the misgivings and the worries, and, ultimately, as for many who feel their tunnels falling apart around them, the psychiatrist. Then the specialist therapists and the sensitivity training and the nude encounters and the love games and the growth centers, and on and on. Nothing changed, of course, until he quit his job. Now he sometimes has worries about where his next meal is coming from, but he keeps talking about a rebirth as if he really knew what that meant. So you see what can happen to a person when he discovers his own "interest."

We know most people are unhappy in their work but that kind of knowledge doesn't really convince us of anything. Certainly it doesn't influence the basis on which children are sorted by a combination of interest and ability into their one-way channels.

The issue of ability is another allocation shuck that requires closer scrutiny. Ability is simply being able to do something well. We convince ourselves, our students, and the parents of students that one should follow his abilities—even into the sewers.

One student I knew at Cuney had amazing skill at numbers. He could add them, subtract them, divide them, and everything else at that level with amazing speed and accuracy. So everybody had him do it all the time. He spent so much time adding columns of a hundred or so numbers that he never got to learn anything else. One progressive teacher thought she could help him read by getting him books about numbers, but that didn't help much because he said reading about them wasn't very interesting. He finally revealed, as a matter of fact, that adding them wasn't very interesting either. He just did it because he was good at that and at practically nothing else. As we all know, teachers look for a student's major strength and then attempt to build bridges to his future for him on the basis of that ability. This particular kid ended up as a clerk in a supermarket and he didn't have to add numbers at all. He had a cash register.

Suppose we were to adopt the alternative perspective on interests and accept the fact that interests and abilities change, that most kids are capable of all, and that no one should be led down a thorny path because at one point in his life he showed an interest or an ability. To solve this problem at the root we would have to change the consciousness of all people, especially parents, and help them see that it is often a mistake to build a life on what you are good at or interested in at one particular moment. If we ground our allocation structure in this kind of understanding we would then shift to a number of substructures or possibilities that would (a) provide for a road back from a false direction and (b) allow students to get involved in activities without requiring that they make a living at it. I knew a man, for example, who was a wonderful cook and spent many happy hours at it. Then, because of the kind of confusion that I am describing, he decided to take a job as a cook; within two months he hated cooking and never did it again. We see these parallels all the time in schools where we ruin a child's love of poetry or music or art by forcing him or her to major in it. A final possibility would be (c) to suggest to children that they choose majors and careers in areas that they find disagreeable so as not to screw up their hobbies and outside interests.

I am definitely not against seeking abilities and nourishing them, but this should be done only if these abilities can be integrated into the child's entire learning experience. This also requires that he be sensitively enough observed so he won't end up doing something well that he'd rather not do at all. Unfortunately, most of the allocation shuck assumes and takes place in the name of "sorting on ability." What really happens is that kids are sorted into pigeonholes (tracks) because that's the way schools are organized: we have to put individuals somewhere.

It's a little bit like saying we have to swat kids because we have a paddle. It's easier to swat them than to get rid of the paddle. It's easier to punish than get rid of all the complicated rules and structures and conditions we've set up to institutionalize corporal punishment. We can't get rid of the death penalty: we've spent so much money building gas chambers, maximum security prisons, and death rows. Capital punishment has become an institution, and people don't vote against institutions even when they're obsolete or destructive.

Frederich Trope was a firm believer in corporal punishment, if the kids were small enough. He always instructed his teachers in the elaborate conditions under which they could hit kids. It took him years to work it out in such a way as to avoid any legal or parental repercussions. I know only one reason he refused to drop the policy, and that had to do with the effort that went into making it up. But this is just an analogy. It often works the same way with abilities.

Part of the problem with abilities is that they are closely linked to patterns of social approval, as I've mentioned above, both for doing special things and for doing anything well. Actually, we are obsessed with this notion. Remember how hard it was to enjoy doing anything in school unless a teacher said you had a real talent for it? I remember I once loved to paint. Every time my teacher came by, she would look at my stuff in obvious disgust. Sometimes, when I would keep at it she would hesitate, just long enough to give me some hope, and then look disgusted again. I was always crushed. Obviously, I stopped painting. That teacher was not exceptional. They're all trained to register disgust, especially with 14-year-old boys who show involvement with anything without demonstrating talent. Obviously I was never allocated into any creative arts classes. I got to take special classes in grammar because I was so good at it. As you can see, I've rebelled.

And so the shuck goes on, allocating kids to classes and activities and curricula that fit their special abilities. Given all we know about job dissatisfaction and generally unhappy lives, you'd think educators would experiment a little bit with putting kids in classes where they show no ability at all. I wish I had been allowed to take auto mechanics. I got a chance to be in electric shop once for about a month, but I flunked out because I couldn't make the damned bell ring. To this day I insist I enjoyed doing the wiring. Why do we always have to make bells ring?

We also have the assumptions surrounding intelligence; that is, that students should be differentiated according to levels of IQ scores. As I've said elsewhere, this is a very destructive shuck. It shucks the teacher into thinking he has some scientific grounds for teaching kids with the same IQ in the same way. It shucks the child into accepting his whole educational destiny by the time he's about ten. It shucks counselors into thinking they are somehow either justified or redeemed, depending on whether or not they ever think about it, when they send one kid to Harvard and another to push racks in the garment district. And it also shucks parents into keeping up hope and punishing kids for not living up to their "potential."

One of the things that happened to George in his up and down career at Cuney High illustrates how the dirty business of IQ sorting works. George had been stuck in the vocational curriculum for about a year at this time. It turned out that one of the reasons he couldn't get out of it was that there was nobody at home to come in and complain. Administrators are much more cautious about allocation decisions when there is somebody in the home who might challenge it. But in George's case, this wasn't so, at least for that period of time. Then his sister came back from Europe, where she had been living with some gypsy film director. She was superbright and superverbal and she took Trope apart to the point where several of us in the outer office wondered if we shouldn't rush to his aid. Anyhow, Trope insisted that she and George speak to the head counselor, who would review the whole case. It became clear Trope would go out of his way to guarantee George got back into college prep as long as the sister was around, but, true believer that he was, he wanted tests to back him up. So the school psychologist was called in with his little bag of measurements.

George got to take another IQ test, this time individually administered. He told me all about it.

Our school psychologist was a very peculiar chap who was always on
the verge of growing a beard, but no sooner was it about a quarter of an
inch long than he'd cut if off and start again about three days later. I
wonder if he ever decided it was OK to let it grow all the way? He wore
baggy black pin-striped suits and frayed collars with a tie that looked
like he'd slept in it. The tie was squeezed about his neck like a clamp,
and he was forever sticking his finger in his collar. He never loosened
his tie.

Anyhow, this was the image that confronted George across the
testing table. He told me every time this guy asked him a question he
would smile without showing his teeth and between the half beard and
the tie and the grin and a few other distractions, George just couldn't
think quickly enough to do well on the first part of the test. At the
half-way point, George told the psychologist he had to go to the
bathroom. He insisted that it was legitimate, that he really had to go, but
he also just had to get away from this guy who was shattering his
nervous system. So what does the friendly guy do? He decided he has to
go too and that they should go together. This made George very
uncomfortable, but he had to go through with it. We always do.

To make matters worse, the psychologist took the very next urinal
and gave George the same wide grin throughout the whole attempt. Of
course under these circumstances, George couldn't go at all. The last
straw in this agonizing experience occurred when James James,
George's bench mate in Mr. Green's shop, came in and started rapping
to George about all sorts of sexual things. George hinted, but James
didn't catch on very quickly since the psychologist was on the other side
and almost out of James's view.

Back at the testing table, five minutes into the testing, George now
felt as if he had to urinate twice as badly as before but he couldn't say
anything because he had just faked one. To shorten this story, George
did very poorly on the IQ test and was sent back to the vocational
curriculum. By this time his sister was back in Europe and the status
quo again prevailed.

By now most of us know that IQ tests are the special province of the
economically affluent. Despite some racist notions to the contrary, it is
apparent to most who are interested that the kinds of cognitive skills
called upon in intelligence testing are those skills picked up in homes

where parents are highly verbal and where abstract realities are more the rule than the exception. When parents talk about responsibility and ambition and achievement and creativity, children also learn to conceptualize in these terms. Their consciousness is developed along lines that allow them to make sense of facts and figures, and eventually the questions that tests ask. Of course the same thing that can be said about IQ testing can also be said about achievement in school in most academic areas. When it comes to dealing with the world as an abstration, give me a well-socialized bourgeois kid every time. If I'm interested in surviving after the H-bomb, well, that's another matter.

School personnel, it turns out, also have problems with the allocation shuck, especially involving those kids who can't be tracked toward something respectable. There is the problem of finding something for them to do, and at the same time making it look like this something is really worthwhile. That is, wherever we put them, we have to shuck everybody into thinking something valuable is happening to the kids. Mainly we have to shuck their parents. The kids know better but we don't really care about what they think, since they have no power to do anything.

So that is the task. Since educators have been doing it for so long, they have become pretty good at it. We have a course like math, and we divide it into several sections. The top section is for the kids who might need it as they go on, the second section is for the kids who will go to work after high school and might use some math where they work. The low section, and kids know which is which, is for those who won't ever use anything but are required to take it anyhow, because that's how schools are organized. In this class, the teacher spends his time figuring out things for the kids to do to keep them from causing trouble. If you walk into a math teacher's room, at least the ones at my school (and many others that I've visited), you can see the whole pattern on the board. It reads something like this:

Classwork:
Period I (top group) *Algebra*, p. 213, problems 1–5. Check answers.
Period II (middle group) *Math*, pp. 271–3, problems 1–10. Check answers.
Period III (dumbbell group) *Arithmetic*, pp. 101–103, Problems 1–176.

The point is that with the dumbbell track you keep them busy, and you don't use up too much of your own energy because you'll need it for the other classes. You give them as much to do as they can manage, but you don't spend too much time talking about things, because talk will just confuse them and, besides, things can get noisy.

All sorts of shucks go on in this tracking system. For example, everybody pretends that one track is just as good as another, but everybody knows it isn't. I know in my own experience, as unenlightened as I was back then, I would have one set of lesson plans for the smart kids, which I worked on diligently, and another set for the dumb track, for which I would devise a week's plan in about ten minutes' time. This would mainly involve activities like looking up hundreds of words in the dictionary, punctuating sentences, grammar exercises by the thousands doing things like "who" or "whom," and plenty of silent reading.

George was an interesting case, since he was in both tracks during the same high school career. He told many revealing stories about differential treatment. His experience in math was that he did hardly any work at all in the smart class and got a B, and got all the answers right on every test in the dumb class and got a C. He told me his math teacher, who was the same for both classes, told him he had to take the competition into consideration in each class, and that it really wasn't fair for him to get an A in the dumb class when the kids in the smart class had much harder work. The B he got in the smart class was simply because he was one of the better students in the school, which was indicated by the fact that he had been allocated to the class.

In George's English class the situation was a little different. In the good track, George told me they did uninteresting stuff like read Shakespeare and analyze sentence structure and read books written in the nineteenth century, like *Silas Marner* and *Lorna Doone*. In the dumbbell-track class it was really interesting, because the teacher let them talk about anything they wanted, since he didn't think English mattered to them anyway. George said that one teacher, who was fired at the end of the year for not being able to control his classes, would just rap about all the things the kids were interested in and they laughed a lot. This isn't the rule though. Usually, the emphasis is on the grammar and dictionary work.

The thing that really grips the mind is the knowledge that it all begins with a couple of achievement tests and an IQ test, and it wouldn't be so tragic except that schools allow something called the "halo effect" to exist. This means that once a kid is tracked, his reputation precedes him from class to class to class and really effects his whole life. Sometimes, as in the case of James James, this halo effect is passed down from brother to brother. In social psychological terms, this turns out to mean that teachers come to expect certain performances of certain kids based upon their reputation from the class before. In turn, kids have to learn to be sensitive to these expectations, and are for the most part forced to meet them. If you expect a kid to cause trouble he usually does, especially since we begin to treat him like a criminal before he's broken any rules. "I know about you James, so you just watch your behavior in this class."

The story of James James is a perfect example of two parts of the allocation shuck, the "halo effect" and the "cool out." The halo effect was a reputation passed down from four older brothers, none of whom made it through the eleventh grade.

Two of James's brothers were in jail at the time. He never knew his father. His is exactly the kind of circumstance that allows the allocation shuck to perform its wonders. James came from elementary school to junior high with the same reputation as all his brothers, and then on to high school with the appropriate junior high recommendations. I was James's tenth-grade counselor, which means that I did grouping things only—putting kids into tracks and taking them out. I never got much of a chance to talk to the kids about their circumstances, but at the same time I don't know if anything I said or did would have made a difference. We soon learn in schools that it's the school that counts, not the people in it. There was little difficulty in assigning James to the vocational curriculum. Since he could barely read or write, we had to conclude that he was good with his hands. If we didn't have that option, we would have needed a new track and nobody at our school knew how to make one, or even if it would be permissible to do so.

In the teachers' room the afternoon of the first day of the new semester the conversation was inevitable. I was trying for the twentieth time to make sense of a magazine called *Auto Mechanics* when one of our more senior faculty exclaimed, "Well, I've got another one."

He said it in the same way he might have said he had another tumor.

"Another what?"

"Another one of the James boys."

"Christ, is there no end?"

"You know how they breed."

"Maybe this one will be different," I offered, tentatively.

"Sure, maybe the next Pope will be Jewish."

Part of the problem was that even if they had been a little more open minded and able to treat each kid as an individual, the tracking system would still lock him in. Combine that with the large number of students we have to process with limited support and few faculty, and it really seems impossible that a different way of relating to students can ever develop. The halo effect gets maximum support from the way we organize our functions in school.

By the end of his first year of high school, James James knew one thing for certain: he had little to lose. Maybe he knew it earlier in his life, but I sense that all kids look to each situation as a possible new beginning. It never works out that way. Once I did a study on the reputation of high school kids as this affected their achievement. I had to use something called the cumulative records, which are a set of records that follow a kid through his school career. Teachers are required, sometimes once and sometimes twice a year, to make entries. This is one responsibility teachers don't seem to take very seriously, judging from the thousands of records I have seen. In one elementary school, a little girl had exactly the same comment made about her by every teacher: "very sweet, respectful, tries hard, does not catch on too quickly." It was like six different teachers saw exactly the same thing. Or did they see it because the one before did?

I followed the careers of some of these students to check out the hypothesis that nice kids go far regardless of ability. This little girl graduated from college. Another little boy whose cumulative record read something like "very bright, must learn self-control, immature," dropped out of high school in the eleventh grade.

James James's record described him as "nervous, immature, slow learner, lacks self-control." About eight of his nine lifetime teachers saw the same human being. The ninth grade teacher thought he should be in a detention camp. This word "immature" is one of those marvelous, meaningless words of description which teachers fall back on when they can't really describe the specific dynamic. It seems to mean, from the best of my searching, that "immature" students lack the maturity to do exactly what they're told when they are told to do it.

Anyhow, James James was immature. In junior high school the P.E. teachers used to allow him to break all the rules in games if he was funny enough about it. From then on, as I was able to piece the story together, James learned that the best way to get along with the white teachers who made impossible demands on him was to amuse them. It seemed to work, especially with Mr. Green. Most of his pranks were harmless and were conducted at appropriate times (not during flag raising) and James was usually pretty good about judging which teachers would be receptive and which ones wouldn't. But every once in a while he got carried away, like the time he slipped into the girls' bathroom for a smoke and got trapped by a bunch of girls who came in from some activity that broke in the middle of the period. As I heard it from George, who heard it from James, one girl who was sitting on the pot in the booth next to his saw the smoke starting to spill over, and tried to see where it was coming from. James said he couldn't help himself, and when the girl's head finally came under the divider he leaned down and kissed her. One scream, then another, and James was ready to be transferred to Weeds.

Weeds High School is the bottom rung of the allocation ladder. It's a school for "immature" boys who require special attention to get them through the age of compulsory schooling. Anyway, James's mother was called in by the vice-principal, whose name was Richard Flail, in order to process the transfer. I was called in for the conference as his grade counselor and the "cool out" shuck was about to begin.

Cooling out is a bit like defusing. It's a way of convincing people that what is being done to them, as atrocious as it may appear, is really in their best interests. It is a kind of mystification, where you convince parents that sending their kids to a work camp is done in order to develop good citizenship in them.

So James's mother showed up in a print dress. She was about 50 and looked 70. She sat down like she was tired and waited for the bad news. Mr. Flail gave her the background, and indicated that "in order to help James learn how to conduct himself in a civilized way we are sending him to a place where they specialize in improving conduct."

There are thousands of students circulating around the city in order that they might learn how to improve their conduct. Parents of kids who get this treatment realize, but usually don't care, that special schools for conduct problems are an educational dead end. It is unlikely that one kid in 10,000 comes back from one of these schools and "fits in" to the old routines sufficiently to improve his chances of graduating from high school. School disciplinarians, particularly vice-principals, have an unspoken code which goes something like, "you take my problems and I'll take yours." The psychology behind this wise strategy is that it takes a kid a few weeks to establish himself in a new school before he secures a base for troublemaking. Once it starts, he's off again to a new environment. So it had been with James's brothers. It was about to begin with James.

"I want's to talk with the head man," Mrs. James told the VP.

"Well," said Flail, "I assure you Mrs. James that this falls within my jurisdiction as vice-principal, and I can certainly take care of whatever it is that you . . ."

"Uh, uh," she cut him off, "no way, not this time, I ain't gonna be wastin' my time wif no flunkie, no 'vice' anything."

I was glad I was only minimally involved.

"I'm sorry," Flail said, asserting himself, "but that is impossible. This is my . . ."

"I knows about you jewisdiction but this time I wants the head man. I got somethin' to say an' he might as well be the one to hear it."

"Now, Mrs. James . . ."

"Uh, uh, you get me the boss or I'ze leavin' right now an' gone down to see the Reveren who tole me that this shit got to stop an' he'll come with me nex time."

Trope was called in immediately. Administrators freeze when community intervention is threatened. I walked Mrs. James next door to Trope's office. We picked up James on the way over.

When we got to Trope's office we deposited James on the bench outside and went in. Trope was a gentleman. He stood until she was seated, then he proceeded to try to make her comfortable. I sat in the background where I could see both of them and also James, who was straining to hear the goings on. Trope then went into his document-consulting phase. School administrators don't like to be caught making decisions without documents. He examined the "facts" for a couple of minutes while we sat in uncomfortable anticipation.

"Mrs. James," he began sympathetically, "You're from the South, aren't you?"

"Louisiana," she said, briskly.

"Yes, yes, I spent some time in the South too. Things aren't too good down there, are they?"

"Good as here," she said.

"No, I mean for black people," he added.

"I means that too," she said.

"Yes, hmmmmm," Trope went back to the documents.

There was a pause.

"Why does the boy do stupid things like that?" he asked her. James got up and took a bow which only I could see.

"Like what?" she asked him.

"Like sneaking into girls' bathrooms and smoking on top of it."

She didn't know.

"Well," he told her, "what you need to do is spend more time with your boy, help him with his work, keep him in nights, convince him that it doesn't pay to be going around fighting everybody all the time."

All the time he was speaking, James was making these funny faces imitating Mr. Trope and I had to keep from smiling. Mr. Trope began telling Mrs. James how he had had the pleasure of having several of her children at his school and he wanted to know how many more he could expect. She said that James was the youngest, and he said that was too bad.

I felt out of the whole thing somehow.

Then Mr. Trope yelled for James to come in and he said, "Your mother and I have agreed that you need firmer discipline."

"I never said no such thing," said Mrs. James, and then there was an uncomfortable quiet.

"What I mean, Mrs. James, is that we agreed we could give James the benefit of our understanding."

"I understand good enough," she said, "through five children that no matter what they do they's gonna take a hell of a beatin' at your high school."

"But I thought we agreed," Trope began, but Mrs. James cut him off again and I could hear James's "tee hee" very quiet.

"We ain't agreed on nothin," she said, "I been waitin for you to finish havin your say and tellin me how you knows us cause you're from the South and all too."

Mrs. James was shouting a bit and Trope sounded like he'd gotten in a little over his head. He was having trouble regaining control.

"Now Mrs. James, please, can't we talk this over calmly?"

"I been calm an watched four of my others get flunked out of your high school and James is the last and and looks like he's on his way out too, now that looks to me like prejudice."

"Prejudice?" Trope gulped. I could see he was dumbfounded.

"Prejudice," she said. "What else can we expect from a southern principal?"

"Southern?" he said with another gulp. "I was three months in basic training in Georgia, I never saw the outside of the camp. Believe me, Mrs. James, I have the utmost respect for the Negro people."

"We ain't no people," she said, and I noticed a couple of the old secretaries standing up and leaning over the counter and one or two teachers getting curious too but pretending to be reading their mail.

"No, we ain't," she went on, "we just trying to get through a no-good high school has it in for all us Jameses and I think it's about time somebody got to talking to the Panthers or NAACP or some group about your school.

"The what? Now Mrs. James. Please. This is getting out of . . . I mean, really, we *are* trying with James, honestly, we are making every effort. James tell your mother."

"I got to be late again," James said, "got three more detentions."

"No," Trope said. "No you don't, they're canceled. It was a mistake."

"Always making mistakes with the James boys, huh?"

"We don't tell them to break all the rules," Trope said. And I couldn't tell if he was defending himself or attacking. "Look, look, ask Mrs. Wilson."

"Don't know any Mrs. Wilson."

"You must. Look, her boy is president of our school. The nicest black boy. We are fair here."

"I suppose you is always fair with the James boys. Now Mr. Principal, I went along with all the others, but now after James there ain't no more and I made up my mind to speak out this one time because five out of five seems to me to be discrimination."

"Good Lord," said Trope.

"Well," said Mrs. James.

"Just a minute, please." Trope told one of the secretaries to call Mr. Flail on the double.

Mr. Flail came in quickly like he always did, holding his thumb behind him. He had a twitching thumb which he held behind his back when he went in to see Mr. Trope.

"Yes, Mr. Flail. Mr. Flail, this is Mrs. James."

"We've met," he said "Good to see you again, Mrs. James."

"I'll bet you believes that," she said.

"What?"

"Mr. Flail, would you say we discriminate here, I mean, you're the disciplinarian."

Flail looked cautiously from one to the other. "You know," he began, "that the school president is black and the head of the PTA."

"So I been told," she said.

Give it up guys, I was thinking. No amount of bullshit is going to convince this old lady of the justice and integrity of Cuney High School.

Flail stood right in front of me, cutting off my view of the proceedings. I had to stretch my head to see, as if I were behind a pole at the ball game. I didn't want to miss anything, particularly since it was obvious that nobody was going to involve me.

Flail took Trope off the hook, as he felt it was his responsibility to do.

"Mrs. James, you must understand that the decision to transfer James to another school is completely mine. Mr. Trope does not get involved in disciplinary matters."

That was a heavy lie.

"Have you thought of sending James to a trade school?" he asked, "there are some good ones we recommend, and a good manual training might just do the trick to help James develop a sense of responsibility."

"Yes," Trope interjected, "good suggestion. And he can be helping earn money for the family."

"Why can't he learn that here?" she wanted to know, since that's what we all knew was supposed to be happening.

"Well," Flail said, "because here there are too many distractions. Other things that he has to get involved in that don't suit his needs, like classes."

"How come nothin' here suits James's needs, or my other boys neither?"

"That's no way to look at it," Trope said defensively. "There are many things here to meet James's needs, he just refuses to see it. We can only help him if he wants to be helped."

Sure, I thought, as long as he is willing to acknowledge that the way we decide to run his life is in his best interests we can help him. I think Mrs. James saw the contradiction as clearly as I did. I wonder if either Trope or Flail had any idea. Flail shifted to a general discourse on how the schools have the interests of the majority of students in mind, and must not allow those few who don't see where their welfare lies to disrupt the process.

"Yes," Trope added confirmation. "You see?"

Mrs. James stood slowly. "Sure I see. Come on along James, we'll just have to wait and see how things go along from here on." She walked out without giving any of us a good-by or even an acknowledgment that the session was concluded.

Trope and Flail stood facing one another somewhat unsure of what had just happened. Trope said to him, "Give the boy a break, will you, Fred? I mean at least he's the last of the Jameses. That's something to be thankful for."

And so I witnessed my first attempt at high-level cool out. Later on, I was to see others where parents with a range of concerns were to become convinced of such things as:

"Your son might not be an engineer, Mr. Smith, but he'll be a good citizen and can do a responsible job working for somebody else."

"Have you considered a junior college, Mrs. Brown? I understand they have excellent programs for slow readers."

"It's not that we're against clubs so much Mrs. Jones, it's just that if Tommy spends all his time protesting these racial issues he'll never make up the work so he can get into a good college."

"I know your daughter would like to be in the college prep course, Mrs. Donaldson, but just look at all of these scores. Look, there's nothing wrong with being a good wife and mother, is there?"

A professor from Berkeley by the name of Clark* once did a study on the junior college system and was one of the first to talk about the "cool out." This was an attitude that noncollege material high school graduates had to have a place to go so they could see they weren't college material. At the same time, students could live with the illusion that

*Burton Clark, "The 'Cooling Out' function in Higher Education," *American Journal of Sociology* (May 1960), 569–76.

they were college students destined for superior things. Only a small percentage of junior college students graduate from a four-year college. As a result of their two-year stint, they are usually crucified in the dilemma that since they have some college, they are above manual labor, skilled or unskilled, and yet they can't compete with four-year college graduates on the labor market.

If there really is an honest function for the junior college, I suppose it is for those who need another chance, having blown their opportunities in high school for access to a good four-year college. I'm not really a critic of junior colleges, except where they are functioning to "cool out" losers. I do worry a bit about the attitude of some JC instructors I've observed. Their own status hangup leads them to intensify academic demands for their struggling students beyond what four-year college professors would demand. But that's another shuck category.

Anyhow, to end the James story, they kept him on in the school for another year, and then he just stopped coming. I don't think anyone tried to find out why. It's just another version of the allocation shuck, to help students meet their needs by having them withdraw from education on their own. Sort of an allocation by default, which is no small matter. Allocation, at the level of an individual's motivation, usually turns out to be a self-sorting business after all, where kids with strong academic backgrounds and motivation simply push their way into the front of the opportunity tunnel, and kids who missed out somewhere just fade away, leaving the struggle to the "fittest."

It seems to me that the way to stop the wheels of the allocation shuck system would be to take away the rewards at the end of each track. I am talking about the certfication that proclaims that one has run a particular race in an approved manner. Like one of the many games that kids know better than adults it might be interesting. to provide a lot of tracks that circle into each other and/or have a lot of bridges from one track to the other. If it's all one degree and no costs to the student from trying things out, we might begin to beat the allocation system, or at least the invidious consequences of being in one rather than another.

The allocation shuck involves a number of rituals along the way. That is, when we sort people, we want to be sure they know where they are, so they don't get into the spaces where other people belong and muck up our program. Put another way, a la Calvin, if you're one of the chosen people, we want to be sure you have your sign, so you will keep on behaving yourself. On the other hand, if you're not going to make it to educational heaven, we want you to know that too, so you don't get presumptuous and start expecting privileges.

Besides the whole grading system, kids get their signs by the associations they are permitted to join. In our high school all the kids on the Yearbook committee got A's in English, even though they never went to class. They knew they didn't have to go. How did they know? They had their sign. In this case, they were allowed to serve on the Yearbook committee.

At Cuney, the vice-principal had his way of giving kids their sign. Flail had a program called "Bum of the Week." It was an alternative status system for kids who couldn't make it the approved way.

Depending on the number of points you got for being sent to the V. P. or the demerits you got in your classes (he conned teachers into sending demerits into his office) you could get into the race for "Bum of the Week," which meant you had a special chair in the V. P.'s office with a sign over your head and your name would be announced in the daily bulletin on Monday. There was also a first runner-up and a second runner-up. A whole subculture of competitors for this honor evolved arond the V. P.'s office.

Once the kids really had their sign from on high, which meant "no chance," they amused themselves with others from the subculture, building their own rituals in opposition to the achievement rituals of the "chosen."

Here is George's way of describing the experience:

Now that I think of it, Mr. Flail's office was one place where I got to feel I belonged. I mean you would always know most of the guys down there, and they would know you and they would kid you like saying, "Where you been, I been saving your seat for you." Things like that. And that gave you the chance to make up a big funny story about how serious your crime was. Even though they knew you were bullshitting they'd really bring you on, and say things like, "No shit?"

One time I told them old lady Spoonstein caught me jerkin off behind one of her poetry books, and that really brought the house down. I was King of the Bench that morning. All I was ever down for though was clowning around in class or being late too often. Mr.

Flail always kept me waiting like he did everybody but he never did much except give me detentions. He told me he thought all things considered I was a pretty nice kid, so why was I such a bum?

With Mr. Green it was always dummy but with Mr. Flail, bum was his favorite word. He even had this big bulletin board in the office and the heading on it was Bum of The Week. Then he'd put down the name of the kid who had screwed up the most in the last week. Some kids thought it was quite an honor, but they found out that if you make the honor roll three times you got sent to Weeds High School, which is strictly survival of the fittest if you know what I mean. That was the greatest threat Mr. Flail had, and he always went through with it because he believed it was very important to his reputation that he never gives in or else everybody will expect him to. I heard him tell this to Mr. Trope and he thought it made good sense.

I was never the Bum of the Week because I just wasn't that bad. James made it once but that was by accident because Mr. Flail had already made up his mind before it was time on Friday afternoon. He didn't think anybody could top James's bit in the girls' bathroom, but some kid did at four o'clock after school which is still counted as part of that week.

Mr. Moody the English teacher had kept some boy, I forget his name now because he was sent to Weeds right after, and this guy must have cracked at the way Mr. Moody kept straightening his tie because he grabbed hold of the tie and was squeezing it tight up against Moody's throat until it was choking him and the kid wouldn't let go even though a couple of other teachers came in and were trying to pull the kid off. I heard the story from one of the guys in my homeroom who was also being kept after school. I would never do anything so serious but I know how you can get to feel with Mr. Moody straightening that tie all the time while he's telling you what a bum you are.

Another reason why it was no good to be named Bum of the Week was because Mr. Flail made you stand by your name during the lunch hour for a whole week so everybody could see who it was if they didn't know your name. Even somebody like James was very embarrassed and you wouldn't think he would be.

Mr. Flail had very curly hair and had been an English teacher but you would never know it from his language. Particularly when he got mad, which he did very often. Sometimes he would be mad from the last kid he saw and it was your bad luck if you went in right after somebody got to him. You could get five detentions for something that you only got one for before. If you were smart and you knew some kid was going to get him mad you'd pretend you had to go to the bathroom very badly and ask the monitor who kept a record of who came in, if it was all right to go to the bathroom. You had to figure that there was a chance of skipping your turn and that by the time you got in to see him, Mr. Flail would have cooled off. It didn't always work out because some days he just stayed mad all day.

Other days he was different, almost smiling and making a joke out of everything, like the way you talked or looked. He'd sometimes make something goofy out of your name like one kid whose name was Peterson he would call Peterhead, stuff like that.

Then there were his creative days. By that I mean he would try to think up brilliant new ways to punish kids. I think he spent his nights thinking them up, also maybe while he was shaving or driving to school. One day he put James in this big wire cage they had on the second floor of the gym that was used for lifting weights and he made James walk around with his arms hanging very low and he would bring a bag of peanuts for whoever was around to throw at him.

I don't understand how anyone would want to be a vice-principal, to spend all your time giving out punishment, you could hire someone without an education for that. Except I guess it's something you have to go through to get to be a principal.

It's not that Mr. Flail didn't talk to you a little bit about what you did to be punished. He'd always ask you why you did it and I never heard anybody say anything but "I don't know." Mainly because when you were caught redhanded what could you say? You could sure hear a lot of "don't knows" while sitting on a vice-principal's bench. It didn't make any difference if you did know, because you always got the same number of detentions, unless he was mad, and then you might get more.

There was only one danger of allocating kids irretrievably to the lower depths, and that was that we might lose all control over their behavior. If, for example, students stopped caring about detentions and swats and expulsions, we were in real trouble. That kind of allocation only works where students retain enough fear of the consequences to control their inclination toward extreme behavior. As every teacher who has ever worked in a nonmiddle-class high school knows, there are always episodes. My most dramatic event occurred when a student named Crazy Gomez, who had gotten his sign years back, along with many of his fellow Chicanos, came into my room looking for George. It turned out that they thought George had told the authorities that Crazy was selling marijuana around school.

As Crazy walked in the door I asked him for a note, but he didn't pay any attention to me. He just walked to George's seat in the back of the room, lifted him up by his shirt, hit him, and knocked him down. Then he told him to get up again. George looked around the room and said, "Hey, fellows" to his classmates.

"Stand up motha fucks," Crazy said.

I told him he wasn't allowed to use words like that in school. I don't know where I suddenly got my morality.

George stood up and tried to defend himself, but Crazy was really crazy. He picked up a big glass bottle from the shelf and started coming toward George. I remember yelling something about school property but Crazy didn't pay any attention.

The other students in the class moved their legs fast so Crazy could get by easy. I started after Crazy, who was after George. Have you ever tried cornering a kid in a room with eight aisles? We ran up and down the aisles and finally George got behind my desk. He and Crazy started playing this game where you try to figure out which way the other is going to go. George was really driving Crazy crazy because he began cursing like wild and his hair was in his eyes and he was sweating, about as much as George was sweating.

George kept saying that it wasn't him whatever it was, but Crazy didn't pay any attention. Then he said that Flail was trying to frame Crazy; he thought about that for a second and I thought George might be off the hook but Crazy changed his mind again.

"You're being framed!" George yelled at him, after they stopped again to figure out which direction around the desk to take. Most of this scene I was observing from the floor, where I had fallen because of somebody's big feet. My leg was killing me.

A few minutes later, Flail came running in with a couple of the gym teachers and I started to relax. Crazy laid the bottle nicely down on my desk and said, "Man, I bein framed," and strutted out, nice and easy. I heard him say as he got outside, "Now you guys just can't do none of that to Crazy. I'm hip to you."

These days more kids than ever have their allocation signs and take what we might consider risks all the time. They beat up teachers, rape girls on the fire escape, steal the principal's car. It seems to me kind of stupid to track kids out of caring much what happens to them early in the game, because we really end up losing our best form of social control, which is that a kid thinks he has something to lose.

Most lower-class kids, mainly from minorities, get their signs in interesting new ways today. They find out, for example, that they are "culturally deprived." This is a way of communicating to a young mind that he has been deprived of a worthwhile upbringing and he's behind the eight ball before he starts. To clean that mess up, educators then stigmatize these students with something called, in true shuck fashion, compensatory education. This is a shuck in several senses. It begins as a way of getting the Board of Education and public-spirited citizens out of the need to integrate their schools. Then it cools everybody out by convincing them that a real opportunity for competitive learning is being given.

As we all know, Headstart and other special programs in segregated ghetto schools just don't do anything to "equalize opportunities." Part of the shuck about "equal opportunity" is to assume that kids who get the same amount of "good" education have an equal chance against each other. But it doesn't work that way. The main advantage of talking about equal opportunities is that it makes suburban liberals feel better about keeping their kids in all-white middle-class schools.

My own assessment of this problem is that it's all pretty hopeless. Nothing short of complete integration and reduction of competitive standards will work. The problem is not in the fact that one group cannot compete for the rewards with another group. It's that education is competitive in the first place. It seems to me rather than go through the messy business of trying to equalize the weight on the horses, we should just call off the race. It's really not very much fun for anyone.

CHAPTER SEVEN

The Management Shuck

Make no mistake about it, the challenge of the classroom is the challenge of discipline. The average teacher thinks when she has learned to control the behavior of every student in her class she has arrived. She has been well conditioned, both by her own educational experience as a student and by her training as a teacher, to demand nothing less of herself. We purport to be such an efficient society, yet it seems to me we would have saved a great deal of time and effort if we had simply gone over to Germany and hired about 40,000 well-trained ex-Nazi storm troopers. Why didn't we take a lesson from the excellent northern states' tactic of recruiting police from the white South, particularly from areas where they have been trained to protect against hordes of wild encroaching peoples of dark skin?

We base our entire law-and-order philosophy in public education on a number of unfounded assumptions. Most of these are supported by the society at large, and by official educators at the top of the school hierarchy. One of these is "If you trust anyone, he'll take advantage of you."

When my youngest child was still attending a public school, when I was still as big a shucker as the rest of the citizenry, she was sent home one day because she had forgotten to bring a note explaining her previous day's absence.

"Hayley," I said, "didn't you tell the teacher you were sick?"

"Sure I did," she replied, "but she didn't believe me."

"What makes you think she didn't?"

"Because she said I had to have a note."

Now, I have always wanted my children to grow up with a sense of trusting others and I would like to have them think people basically trust them, so they don't have to spend half their lives proving that they're trustworthy. I went to speak to the teacher.

I first went to the office, as the rules require, and said I wanted to see Hayley's teacher. The secretary said she thought it could be arranged, but that she would have to see if there was another teacher free to watch the class while the teacher talked to me.

"I'll only be a few minutes," I said. "I don't see why you need another teacher."

"Oh no!" she gasped, aghast at the image of a class without a teacher. "We can't leave the children unmonitored."

I decided to play out the whole drama as if I were a visitor from another planet. Of course I knew all their stock answers and understood the consciousness behind them, but I took a sick delight in seeing the whole thing played out bit-by-bit before my muckraking eyes.

"Why not?"

"Well," she started, and then paused to see if I were kidding. I kept a straight face.

"They could just tear the place apart."

I acted as if I were surprised. "What do you mean?" I said. "They're only children."

I was over the hump. She decided to take me seriously. "Oh no," she reemphasized, "you can't leave them alone. They're so nervous."

"Oh," I said, as if I were finally understanding. "I had no idea."

"You ought to try being in a classroom with 35 of those wild Indians," she explained patronizingly, "you'd soon get the message."

I smiled sheepishly to show I was acknowledging my ignorance, and she benignly let me off the hook. She told me to wait on the bench till she returned with the teacher. Again I got the feeling there was a very definite atmosphere of distrust in the building.

About five minutes later she approached with a young, stacked, bleached blonde who shook my own stereotype system. The secretary introduced us and we sat down on the office bench to talk. I got right to the point.

"I understand you don't trust my daughter."

She looked at me in wide-eyed amazement, as if she had never distrusted anyone in her whole life. I mentioned the absence note. She looked relieved. "Oh that. Well that's just a school requirement. It doesn't mean we don't trust her. Your daughter is a very sweet girl. Of course I trust her."

"Well, when you tell her she can't come back to class without a note from her parents saying exactly why she was out, what is she supposed to think?"

"Well, just that we have rules, I would think."

"Don't you see" I said, beginning to preach "how she would begin to get the idea school is a place where they don't trust children?"

She didn't see at all. "It's just a rule," she repeated.

"I see," I said, deciding to try a new tactic. "Well, perhaps the rules need to be changed. Especially the one which says the child must bring a note."

"Oh," she said, suddenly having figured something out. "But don't you see, if we trusted the kids in that way, some of them would take advantage."

"I see," said I, standing to leave. There was no question about it, I had to find another kind of school for my child.

"If you trust people they will take advantage"; therefore what we need to do is build a system of distrust in order to control the behavior of those who might take advantage. The fact that most kids wouldn't take advantage, even if we started with trust from the beginning, does not seem to enter into the issue. Educators are paranoid about children in general. It is one thing to have a system of punishments for persons who violate certain expectations. It is another to institutionally manage the lives of all as if at every moment they were potential violators.

The behavior of both school secretary and the teacher, an accurate barometer of the consciousness of school environments, communicated a system of thought and a level of role performance that painfully brought home to me the pathetic conditions under which young human beings grow up: that is, in the constant presence of adults who do not trust them.

The alternative to the structure of distrust in schooling is, of course, the opposite: a structure of trust. What would that look like? It would mean supervision of children to protect their health but permissiveness in almost all other matters. It would mean that children could "get away with" nothing because they were free to do anything that did not hurt or impinge upon others. This structure exists in free schools and even in many open classrooms in public schools. The whole assumption is that children have the right to make their own choices, including the choice to get involved in the learning activity or with materials in learning centers which are often part of open classrooms. A consciousness of trust is one that has to permeate all parts of a system so as not to detract from those parts which do operate on trust. This is more than a humane consideration; it is a fundamental educational reality that persons take more chances in a trusting environment than in a distrusting, punative one. Learning, as I see it, requires risks, trying new things, taking chances. Most schools, as we know them, are not places where kids, or teachers can try very much that is new or different; thus learning possibilities are limited.

Another assumption most educators live by is that "We are producing good citizens." Ask any teacher why he invokes all the rules of discipline in the classroom and he will likely reply in a mode very prevalent in our society, that of mystification; that is, by justifying bad behavior for so-called good reasons. "Yes, well . . . it's too bad we have to be so harsh, but they must learn to respect the rules and values of society if they are going to make a satisfactory adjustment to the real world when they get out there." Producing good citizens is almost exclusively defined as manufacturing a generation of people who have a cowering respect for the Rules. Other conceptions of being a good citizen, such as standing up for the Bill of Rights or fighting attempts to dedemocratize our society, are, of course, never considered.

Why do we do these terrible things to children? Why do we distrust rather than trust them? There are several possible responses to this question. One is that distrust is not terrible at all, but is called for by either the nature of the beast we are training or the solution to the problem for which we are training them. The first says something about what we think of our children, the second reveals how little we know about alternative ways of creating or being "good" citizens.

Another response is to suggest the problem lies in the extent to which the public is willing to invest in public education. This notion raises a number of considerations. The conclusion to all of them is that we don't take schools nearly as seriously as we take wars or space exploration or administration. Consequently we end up with millions of groups of 1 teacher and 35 kids—too many to trust—in small, confining, prisonlike spaces.

A third response has to do with the kind of support we give to uplifting (or humanizing) the teaching profession, and ultimately the quality of school administrators, and this has been already touched upon in the chapter on professionalism. In this context, however, it would seem to me one way we can get teachers who do not fear and distrust children is to improve their skills and increase their motivation to become professionals. Improving salaries and recruiting an increasing number of men would be a beginning. At least it would begin to make teaching a much more human profession for the women involved.

Another way of viewing the question/problem is to point the finger at parents, calling upon them to pay attention to the possible harm schools are doing to their kids and suggesting to them that their own values in the home and at work are simply being played out in the schools with their children as multiple victims. I am talking about the values put on possessiveness, distrust, manipulation of others, the definition of all the world as in competition with me. Most parents are very, very ignorant of these dynamics, and very defensive as a result. Which means most of them probably can't be changed. But at least we ought to try, which means initiating an intelligent way of making parents partners in the educative process. This will require techniques of sensitizing them to the dynamics of distrust and the part they play in maintaining it. Of course, as things now stand, we can't get the public to support the building of a new toilet room in a school much less supporting parent-sensitivity programs. My only point is that the techniques are available and the work can be done. Unfortunately, this would cost money and necessitate a massive redistribution of energy and thus is remote. If there were only some way to relate the task to the war effort—if the pentagon were interested, we might stand some chance of instituting these changes.

The government of this nation, and therefore the entire society, is currently obsessed with "law and order." Although this is not the place to investigate the dynamics of the phenomenon, it is important to remember that the public school system has always supported such a policy. In the absence of the ability to meaningfully integrate students into the school experience, we coerce them into participating by threatening them with a wide range of tortures. As I mentioned earlier, we used to use the swat for the younger boys and detentions for the older ones. When problems were becoming too much or occurring too often for us, our vice-principal Flail, would call for Three-detention Day or Three-swat Day. "The first one in," he would say, "give him three and let him go. It'll get around." It always did. So we had law and order by rumor.

I taught in a junior high school for awhile, and that is where law and order really get out of hand. The problem there is that junior high school kids are old enough to make trouble, but not old enough to quit school or be forced out. All the time I was teaching there I felt like a cop. The principal was much more concerned about my hall duty and yard duty and after-school patrol than my composition classes. The special thing about Corpi, a pudgy Italian ex-P.E. teacher, was that his "law and order" applied to the teachers as well as to the students. He patrolled the teachers to make such they were patrolling the kids.

I'll never forget the time I had sidewalk duty after school. My job was to make sure the kids cleared out as fast as possible and didn't violate any school rules until they were about two blocks down the street. Corpi himself would walk around like a nervous father at a birth, always sniffing for smoke or listening for dirty words, or watching for a boy to put his hand on a girl's behind. I was just sort of looking around without wanting to spot anything. Corpi came up to me and gave me a lecture right then and there about my responsibility to keep these kids out of trouble. "But Mr. Corpi," I said, "if I don't spot them, they won't be in any trouble."

He had no sense of humor. He told me to stay at my post until 3:30 today because he thought it was going to rain and everybody knew kids had to be watched more carefully when rain was coming on.

Trope was much the same, except since the kids in his school were a few years older, he trusted them after they left the school grounds, but not while they were still on it. He allowed most of the older teachers the freedom to keep the kids silent in their own way. Sometimes, though, when visitors showed up, he kept them away from my room on purpose, since my classes usually made more noise then most. I guess he figured it was easier to walk in another direction than to try to change my style. Not so, Mr. Corpi, the junior high man. He walked into my class at least once a day. At one time I thought it was because I had the worst kids, but I found out later that he spent most of his time in the classrooms of teachers who had "new" ideas.

Another brief section from George's biography of Cuney High School gives more of the student's perspective of the law-and-order game. Kids were not necessarily the most adversely affected. At least they didn't take school so seriously. But for the teachers, law and order was a life's work. George begins with his analysis of the librarian and goes on to more general things.

When your class went to the library, Miss Burrows wouldn't let you get out of your seat without giving you a long talk on how you should have a lot of respect for property and that people worked very hard making things nice for us like books and tables and things and that we should respect their effort. But one day in library class she tore up all these beautiful maps from the United Nations and threw them in the wastebasket where she said they belonged. She said that the United Nations was going to get us all in a terrible mess if we let them, but I'm sure they must have gone to a lot of trouble getting those maps to look good and she didn't respect their effort. She also took a lot of books off the library shelf and threw them in the wastebasket because she said it would corrupt us and they were just the ones everybody wanted to read and I hadn't gotten to most of them yet. If books with dirty words or something got her upset she should have said that, instead of telling us that she didn't want us to be corrupted, which couldn't have happened anyhow and I'll bet she knew it.

Everybody was always telling you they didn't see there was anything wrong with something you wanted to do but you couldn't do it since there was a rule. They would never tell you why you had to do something except that you had to because of a rule or because it was good for you. I don't think they thought it was good for you at all, they just had to say it. Take chewing gum. Nobody let you chew gum but everybody did it. Most teachers would say it bothered the class but I never met a kid who said it bothered him. Some teachers would only say that it was a rule and they didn't have to explain it to you. A couple of teachers, Mr. Green for one, said maybe it was a good thing if it helped you work but he didn't make up the stupid rules. Most teachers just pointed to the wastebasket and you had to walk up and grab a piece of paper, wrap it up, and dump it. Everything stopped while this was going on and sometimes, like if it was James James on his way to the basket, it could take a couple of minutes. I bet if you counted all the minutes that teachers waited for kids to throw their gum away, it would add up to another year of school. Some teachers counted the times you were sent to the wastebasket and then sent you off to Mr. Flail the next time you were caught. Mr. Flail was one who admitted that he didn't think it was so terrible but as long as you got sent to him you had to take a couple of swats or detentions. And detentions. If you want to know, they're no good either. Nobody ever changed because he got detentions. But I guess that's alright because they never tell you it will do you any good anyway.

There were lots of things teachers did that were supposed to be helping you get ready to take your place in the world. That was a top expression teachers used. But most of those things were something that just helped the teacher. Like using those grammar books. We used them four times a week and nobody ever learned anything from them. We were just checking verbs and pronouns all day, but it sure made it easy for Mr. Moody, who only had to walk around the room and get a little exercise. Sometimes he didn't even walk, as long as everybody was quiet and looked like they were marking verbs and things. I'll bet they think we never figure out what they're up to.

Mr. Trope liked it when classes were quiet. He would just walk around the halls and listen in and if he heard any noise he would jump in the room. I watched him do it a couple of times. One time we had a student teacher in Mr. Harris's history class and she used to teach the class and Mr. Harris would sit in the back. Sometimes he fell asleep but the student teacher wouldn't let us wake him up. She would just wink at us and put her finger over her lips. She was very nice. Once she let us work in groups on a project she had us doing which was very interesting and kind of fun too, getting to talk to other kids in class, even if we were only talking about the work.

Mr. Trope came jumping in our room shouting, "What's going on here?"

The student teacher who was sitting with one of the groups jumped and said, "We're working on our government projects, Mr. Trope."

Mr. Harris woke up then but he was kind of old and never got very excited. He just listened to Mr. Trope and the student teacher talking back and forth.

"Working, projects," Mr. Trope said, "it just sounds like a lot of noise to me."

"It's not noise, Mr. Trope, everyone is talking about the work." She had a lot of guts, I'll tell you.

"Work is work and talking is talking," he said. "And talking is noise and how can anybody learn anything with all that noise going on?" I think she would have said something but I don't think she could figure out what to say. She just stood there scratching her head and the next day we were all back in straight lines again and our chairs were nailed to the floor. Mr. Trope must have had it done during the night.

Anyhow, as bad as I think most of the teachers were, I have to admit that I didn't play it very smart by going along with them like most kids do. I probably could have made it through if I went along and stayed in the academic course and then maybe I wouldn't have remembered so many lousy things about the school.

But like I was saying, even though I was in the industrial arts curriculum, I was really trying there for awhile and doing pretty well but it was taking a long time to get people around the school to think about how I had changed because I suppose that's a hard thing to believe about people once they've screwed up a lot. Especially when teachers like Mr. Moody had you in class and would always say things like "leopards never change their spots" and "what's the use?"

"Kids never change": that's another major assumption educators make in their management game. The best way to control the whole pack is to watch the troublemakers and as soon as one acts up, out he goes, either home or to another school. School careers are built upon one or two bad years. And it's hard for a kid to ever turn himself about, mainly since the school management game is at least in part built upon the sort-out-the-bad-ones philosophy. Gas chambers are not very sympathetic; school systems are not very forgiving. The point of the mismatch sentence is that our management game, like so many of our inane routines, just does not permit the human element. We are all forgiving, of course, and we are ready to grant any well-meaning soul another chance for salvation, except, unfortunately, it's usually by that time out of our hands. Flail once said to me, "Look, I like the kids and I'd really like to see them get a break, but that's not what we're here for. School is a mass production business and when a bad one shows up, we have to junk it, for the benefit of the rest."

This notion leads us to an obvious conception of an alternative. When, in Chapter Ten, the efficiency model of education is described we can see the industrial parallel. School is like a factory, and for good reasons. If we were not worried about mass production we could solve our humanistic problem. For some hints as to what the alternative would look like we have to retreat in history to a nonindustrial period when education was family based and children learned individually from their parents, who probably cared for them and took great pains in guiding their learning. If we can't afford small group and individualized instruction because we desperately need to contain communism all over the world or because we need to explore distant solar bodies, perhaps we could call on the parents and friends of schools in the community for help. Surely there must be some spark of concern for the individual child in schools, otherwise why insist on only 35 kids per teacher, why not 70 or 700? All over the country, in scattered spots, the community as a resource is making this kind of difference. Again, like so many other solutions it turns out that volunteer help just holds back the time that national monies are redistributed for the greater good of American children. But, nonetheless, I cannot blame those conscientious school people who have turned in desperation to their communities to make up for the resources their country, state, or city cannot spare for their children's education.

Another part of the management shuck is protecting kids from ideas which might confuse them, both because they are only children and cannot be allowed choice and because they are not trained as teachers are, to choose only subjects that contain real wisdom. Perhaps that's going a bit far, for teachers are not allowed that freedom either. The problem is usually solved by putting administrators in charge of all content circulated to tender, inexperienced minds. Sometimes principals allow librarians, if they're sure they are old enough or at least churchgoers, to do a little censoring—to sort out books which contain smut from those which are spiritually uplifting. As most of us know, school libraries are much like magazine stands in small town railroad stations; even though it's one of the most widely read publications today, you can't even get a copy of *Playboy*.

School administrators are often paranoid. They have to be. So much has to be controlled, and unfortunately a good many of those humans who they think need to be controlled are not really willing to accept control when it comes. It's not like managing 40 musicians in an orchestra. Those people want to cooperate.

My own feeling was that Frederich Trope was unusually paranoid, but other teachers I've talked to are always one-upping me about their own principals. The function for all of them is to anticipate where trouble might be coming from and clamp down before it gets started. This requires a military mind and I've never understood how school administrators who came up through the ranks as teachers ever got that kind of training.

Trope was basically an ignorant man although his colleagues and some of his teachers were willing to grant that he ran a "tight ship." My suspicion is that, in order to run a "tight ship" one has to be constantly anticipating a threat to the stability of the organization. Trope was "right on" in that area. His ignorance ran deep and broad. He was just about equally uninformed in most areas. In the area of literature or drama his knowledge was less than minimal. When it came to book purchases he completely trusted Miss Burrows, our librarian, whose distrust of both children and anything new was at least equal to his. So he was relieved of needing to exert much energy anticipating trouble from subversive books infiltrating his library. In the area of drama he was a bit more cautious. We had a drama teacher by the name of Mr. Cranberry with whom I worked as an assistant during my last year at Cuney High. If I had stayed in high school teaching, I probably would have moved into the drama area as quickly as possible. I always felt that there was less of a need to control kids in that class. If you give kids parts to play, they usually wait their turn to play them. It's when kids are unclear about what roles they are expected to play and dislike the ones they are sure of, that they feel pressure to do something inappropriate.

Anyhow, Cranberry was a very sweet man who pretty much played it both ways. He tried to please both the kids and the principal. Trope required that Cranberry submit to him the name of the play he intended to put on each year so he could approve it. Everyone knew Trope would shuttle anything of that nature off to Miss Burrows for her inspection.

Cranberry was a nervous man, about 50 years old, with very little hair. This he tried to grow long. Everybody liked him and felt sorry for him, mainly because he was so nervous about getting Trope's approval every year and there was a standing story about how Trope would pull the rug out from under him two years out of three.

The story I got from the old timers was that after Trope gave the go-ahead and Cranberry and his class had gotten into production, working very hard, Trope would usually have a change of heart and decide the topic of the play, whatever it was, was too controversial. The year before I got involved, Trope was willing to let the play be put on, but insisted at the last minute that the parts be changed because the lead boy was black and the lead girl was white. There wasn't even any romance, but Trope told Cranberry to make the change at practically the last minute. Cranberry had a way of telling his students his problems so as to draw great sympathy from them and they would go along without making a fuss. There were a lot of rumors that there would be trouble and a couple of parents came in, but it was all cooled out for the "good of the community." First he changed the black guy's part to a white guy but ended up changing the white girl's part to a black girl. By the fall, everyone had forgotten the incident except Mr. Cranberry, who was already looking forward to the next play.

The next year we were going to do *Our Town*, which seemed neutral enough. I was in the class to learn, and, for me, it was one of the more profound experiences of my teaching career. The first thing we had to do was wait until Trope had made his inspection and after checking things out with Miss Burrows and being satisfied that we wouldn't bring the race question up again, he gave us the go-ahead.

We worked like hell for about a month and then Cranberry and I got the call from Trope. For Cranberry it was happening again. For him it was like waiting for a bomb to fall and hoping it wouldn't but knowing it would. We went down to Trope's office together. Cranberry kept pushing his few hairs behind his ears and trying to act like it was routine; it probably was routine, but not the kind you'd want to deal with constantly. He joked nervously with the secretaries, who had witnessed the scene several years in a row. Poor Cranberry, was about to get turned round again. They tried to keep his spirits up but we all expected the worst.

Trope kept us waiting just long enough to make us sufficiently ill at ease but not so long that we would get angry. Then he asked us in.

"Cranberry," he began, "we're living in an age of urbanization."

Cranberry waited and then looked at me and then back at Trope. He didn't know what to make of it. I had a hunch.

"This play of yours," Trope went on, "small town, right?"

Cranberry nodded in a pained mannei. He too had caught on.

"Way in the past, right?"

"Yes, but Mr. Trope, that really shouldn't . . ."

Trope cut him off. "What do you think, Weinberg?"—looking to me for an acknowledgment that he was on the right track.

"Yes," I said, "it is about small town folk and a bit in the past, but the message is current."

He looked back at Cranberry as if my comment was irrelevant. "Can't you find something more up to date, modern? This is the age of specialization and modernization, technology!"

I was wondering if this might not be the right moment to suggest that he give me permission to stop teaching Shakespeare in my English class.

"Well, we could, Mr. Trope, but we've come so far . . ."

"No," Trope said, as if he had rethought it and come out with the same conclusion. "We can't retreat to the past. We owe the American people our commitment to keep up with progress. Our men are going to the moon," he said, proudly. He was a superpatriot. I looked at Cranberry. He was biting his lip.

For a tense moment I thought he was finally going to tell Trope to shove it, but he didn't. He decided to try reason one more futile time.

"Mr. Trope," he began, "the students are almost ready. They have worked hard, we don't have any blacks touching any whites or vice versa. I don't think it would be wise to make a change at this point."

132 EDUCATION IS A GREAT BIG SHUCK

Trope stood up and walked around his desk, leaning back against it, very relaxed, very cool. "I know how you feel, Cranberry," he said, showing great concern. "And I would like to stand behind you in this thing, against my better judgment. But we principals are not free to do that. We must be sensitive to the needs of the community and live up to their expectations for us. We have to give them what they want and they don't want a story about a bunch of small town yokels."

"Mr. Trope," I interjected, "*Our Town* is not about farmers. There are broader issues."

"I know the play, Weinberg," he snapped at me. "I do some reading now and then. We just need to be more up to date, more with it."

"But we teach Shakespeare to our senior classes." I finally came out with it.

"That's different," he said, walking back around the desk. "It's in the curriculum."

We were both silent.

"Can you get a modern play?" he said to Cranberry.

"How about *West Side Story*?" I said, "We could have the blacks play the Puerto Ricans."

Trope shook his head. "No racial stuff or anything sexy. Just something up to date and pleasant. Remember, it's for the parents."

"Yes, Mr. Trope," Cranberry said.

I don't know how the students took the bad news because I had my counseling hour at the moment Cranberry announced it. About a week later they submitted a less "controversial" play to Burrows, by way of Trope, and got a new go-ahead. I withdrew because of other responsibilities. Cranberry had the last word though, before he left Cuney High for places unknown. All those parents were sitting in the audience and Trope had on a new suit and tie. All were waiting for the curtain to go up. But it never did. Neither Cranberry nor anyone else in the drama class showed up. I don't know what happened to Cranberry, but the class all got suspended even though they all brought sick notes from home. The only thing I really regret was that they hadn't let me in on it.

To this day I gather great delight in recalling this episode and the first really rebellious teacher I ever met. I never knew Cranberry's home situation, but I assume he had something to lose by turning on his "leader." Most teachers do, which is why they allow the administration to manage everything with little input or challenge.

Before deciding that everything would be different if we just fired all administrators, however, it is important to realize that administrators are themselves mainly just guards, bound by the "rules." The laws and assumptions under which students are managed and controlled have existed for decades. The management consciousness generally has the support of most school personnel because it makes life easier in both the short run and the long run. It is not the teacher who arbitrarily takes responsibility for disciplining and exercising authority over the child, it is a very old rule, which requires that she assume that responsibility or perish. Many a young teacher has not survived her first year simply because she was "unable to control the children."

School is a culture, which means that the things people do is what people before them have done. One learns the way from others who have been there before, and back we go to a time no one can recall. It is not only that we follow and uphold the rules, but that we don't even know things might be otherwise. Culture is a way of viewing the world, and most persons are encapsulated in a certain culture in the sense that they are unable to conceive that the way things are might be changed. Take the idea, for example, that students control teachers and teachers control administrators. Preposterous. Absurd. We have our tradition. Or consider the idea that students can come when they please, stay as long as they desire, and leave when they are bored. Ridiculous. Nonsense. Can we consider the possibility that students choose their own content, their own evaluation system, and their own rewards, and promote themselves and each other in ways they see fit?

Obviously I am not talking about education or schooling. I must have something else in mind, a new culture and new institutions. As things now stand, students must be managed because that is the version of schooling we have inherited and that is the way we see the world. Another version of control and management would require a cultural revolution of the sort that would cause most middle Americans and those who tell them how to live to be sick, both from anxiety and disgust, because the kind of new culture required to supplant the old version of schooling is one that would emphasize spontaneity and deemphasize control or management. It would require teachers to encourage students to do the unpredictable. Can you imagine sitting before a class in full knowledge that you have no idea what is going to happen next? It is a revolting idea, of course—a poor substitute for the exciting daily routines that most teachers now experience.

The Western world is obsessed with the notion of security. The people spend their lives seeking and maintaining it. They don't want anything unpredictable to happen to them. That is why they take out insurance policies. They surround themselves with others whose behavior they can predict, and avoid the company of those of whom they are unsure. They build monuments to stability and put fences around them. Then they stand, mouths agape, when their children walk away from it all. Getting off the treadmill, or escaping the control structures of everyday life, can only be accomplished by those who either can handle the unpredictable or who see the value of trying. When I have my own school, and I hope it will be soon, I only want teachers who will look into the face of insecurity and uncertainty and hold on, knowing they will somehow work it through. For only in this way are we teachers who can let children be themselves, and thus learn in the way that is best for them. Each child is different, and the determination of the management shuck is to deal with them as if they were all the same.

In my own career as a college professor, I have had to struggle with these same issues. The culture of the campus is as controlling as the elementary school, with only one major exception. It's easier for students to walk out the door. This is not a terribly important exception, because walking out the door means walking out on security—the security represented by a college degree, and particularly the extra security of the graduate degree. With this knowledge in hand we shuck students into believing that they are generally more free than their younger brothers and sisters. My guess is that they are even less free. A person almost to the summit of a mountain has more to consider in giving up than somebody way down below.

College students are fully aware they don't have to do it. The only things they have to fear if they should walk away is rejection by their families, the disapproval of friends, and a life of economic unpredictability. Recognizing the cost of nonconforming, most college students thus will do almost anything they are told by anyone in authority. Of course the control structure is a bit more distant than it is in lower-level schools. At the university, the control structure is a set of regulations both for behavior and academic mobility. It emanates from God knows where and is administered by persons students usually only see on closed-circuit television during campus crises.

The prime shuck exists in the unspoken assumption that there are good reasons for the requirements binding college students. There are good reasons for 180 units, for a year of foreign language, for taking the top 5 percent on the college entrance exams, for requiring term papers, for reading a required number of books, for taking mid-terms and finals, for taking lecture notes, for not permitting students to grade themselves, for requiring students to be in residence regularly, for large classes, and on and on.

As faculty, we are, of course, victims of similar controls. We can't even blame administrators. We sit in faculty meetings or in our offices and make up our own suffocating requirements. We have criteria for promotions even administrators can't loosen up, and I sometimes suspect they would like to do so. I am talking particularly about such things as community service and good teaching. My colleagues are myopically impaled upon their conventions of scholarship, and we are all managed by a mythology they have created and will maintain against all intrusions. Of course we do it all on the shuck grounds of maintaining high standards. But what they really do is maintain those below them in positions of groping insecurity, which might be useful if there were other ways out of insecurity besides meeting standards set by superiors.

Last summer I worked with incoming freshmen and their parents in an orientation program. The main question both groups came to ask and to get some understanding of was "How do you survive in college?" I felt my function was to help orient these kids to the ways they might have a good experience and possibly even learn something worthwhile. Clearly we were operating at cross-purposes.

It turns out that the real purpose of the orientation program, and I would suspect this to be true in most colleges, was to do just what the kids and their parents wanted it to do, which was to help them learn how to survive. They weren't even talking about prevailing anymore, just surviving.

The parents were just as anxious as their kids. At least half a dozen parents came to me in private and confided that their son or daughter was sensitive and psychologically frail. Would college destroy them? Could I reduce their anxieties? Of course not. It was all I could do not to increase them.

Students are managed by their fears and their need to succeed, and there is no time to be concerned about other purposes. The only answer I could give these parents created a glazed and pained expression on their faces. I told them, "Your children will be destroyed to the degree that either you or they need to succeed." The whole management shuck would topple like Humpty Dumpty if people only got to appreciate failure more. You can't tell a kid to do something that nearly destroys him if he knows he can handle the consequences of not doing it. Higher education hasn't improved much in the area of making it easier for students to pursue their own interests in a way that doesn't destroy them because there has been no need to improve, as long as college students think their total egos and lifelong hopes are on the line. The only way any institution changes in this or any other country is when the peope are willing to live without the rewards that it offers. That day is not likely to come soon.

One thing the orientation program showed me is that kids see a little bit better than their parents, what the dynamics really are. Parents for the most part think kids should do everything they're told since *we* know what's best for them. Students also believe they should do what they're told, but at least they don't pretend it's because we know best or that it's intrinsically in their best interests.

Some parents are willing to change, are willing to let their children make their own way. Another question the parent group brought up time and again was, "What can we do to help our kids?" Most of them meant help our kids to survive. Some of them understood there is a difference between getting an education and getting a degree. My advice always assumed the former although I realize that most parents meant the latter. I told them to trust their kids, to let them fail, to clarify their own expectations, to deal with the money issue out in the open. Of course I found myself in some arguments. One parent told me it was not his kid's business to know the family's financial situation. "It's enough," he said, "to know that we're sacrificing, and that there are other things we could do with the money."

Students are controlled, then, by the fact that their parents are sacrificing to send them to college. What they do, they do as boys and girls paying off a debt. One parent said, "We want our child to understand that the money isn't important, it's the education that is the only consideration." Doesn't that sound like a liberated parent?

"Fine," I said, "would you give your daughter the same amount of money if she wanted to travel around the world?"

"No," he said, "if she wanted to play around that would have to be at her own expense."

"But suppose your daughter really believed she could get a better education traveling around the world than by going to college?"

"That's silly," the mother replied.

"Well then," I said, to the group at large, about 20 parents, "how many of you are paying the bills?" They all raised their hands. I suppose they had to even if they weren't.

"OK," I said, "what will you pay for and what won't you pay for, and why? What is your child's education?"

They seemed to agree that they all meant formal education. I then indicated that there were formal schools out in the world where one doesn't get a degree. They then agreed they would pay only for that education which would count toward a college degree. I suggested that the act they were really performing was the purchase of a college degree through the bodies of their children. Many agreed they would purchase as many as their children "wanted." Any other kind of education would be "frivolous."

One father who was sympathetic to what I was saying and willing not to turn it all off like the others, pursued it. "What do you mean, 'deal with the money issue with the kids?'"

"Tell them," I said, "just how much a problem the money outlay is and let them know just how much you expect in return. What is the return you desire?"

"All I want," a soft-spoken mother agreed, "is for my daughter to be happy and learn whatever she wants."

"Even if it means that she doesn't get a degree, or she takes six years to get a B.A., or goes to Europe to learn?"

"I think so," she said. "I've just never thought of it like that."

Of course not. If an education were an education and not a carrot, we couldn't control students the way we can. Everyone who has ever worked within a reward and punishment system understands that. The management of others in our society is purely an external gratification concept. As soon as you let people switch to an internal gratification system, you lose control over them. No one is going to continue striving for your carrot when they discover they have one of their own inside them.

There are many points at which the control shuck requires authority figures to come together to control young people. The way parents shuck here is that they say they are sacrificing for their children's educations when they really mean they are buying a little more control over them. If this were not the case, parents would lay the money in front of the kids and say it's yours to get an education anyway you like and in any terms you decide upon. We don't do that. Rather we buy them the kind of education we believe in, which restricts their movements for at least four more years. If we just gave them the money they might cut out, thereby robbing us of a few year's additional dominance over their lives. This attitude feeds into the control structure of the college, because kids who have not yet learned they have some rights in the home are certainly not going to expect any on the campus.

In real terms, this means children who can't make it on their own are not going to chance failure anywhere. And if there is one principle that I believe in with respect to learning, it's that you have to risk failure in order to successfully learn anything. By providing a structure where students do not risk failure (taking courses that might be too tough, writing a paper that excites you rather than one which pleases the professor, answering exam questions your way rather than the way in which you think you'll get the best grade), we guarantee institutionalized performance rather than individualistic learning. And that too pleases most parents, because individualized learning sometimes leads to life styles that are different from those parents have mapped out for their children.

Unfortunately for almost everyone, schools have adopted the consciousness of industry in the way they manage personnel. Some of you may be able to imagine occupations that hold out rewards other than money or external benefits and may even be able to point to a person here or there who would do that work at starvation wages, but this is not the norm. How many college students do you think would continue their "educations" if we started giving out gratis Ph.D.'s?

One of the more interesting dilemmas for many of the parents of incoming freshmen I met with last summer was the one that juxtaposed this consciousness (that students should do anything they are told for the big carrot) against their knowledge that the big university had a lot of radicals on its faculty or in key positions as teaching assistants. Here was one evil they were willing to accept and always had (selling a soul for a degree, on the grounds that "that's the way the world is") and another evil (radical teachers) they wanted to avoid at most costs. Not all, mind you, because I gave them that option: "Would you rather have a child who was exposed to all those radicals who ended up with a degree or one who refused to be exposed and dropped out?" I understand there are more possibilities, but just to tap the limits of their attitudes, I raised the question in this way. Their responses were mixed. Of course we were dealing with a fictional fantasy all the while, which we tried to clarify, but I'm not sure we succeeded to everyone's satisfaction.

The truth of the matter as I see it is that outsiders have a very unreal perspective on the social and political stances of college professors. There are very few radicals as they picture them, and the few who do exist don't politicize in the classroom. But even if they did so, it wouldn't matter a great deal, since students, for the most part, don't attempt to relate ideas to their own lives. That's not the way they've been trained. They mostly want to understand just enough to be able to succeed on examinations. This gets back to the original point about how we manage college students. Their lives are controlled to the extent that they want the degree, and nowhere does this require that students show interest, question their own values, or believe their teachers.

The orientation program, as I look back upon it, was a point at which all our shucks were aired and we were allowed to look at each other's expectations for the forthcoming experience. As the discussion became more honest we all started talking about the realities as we saw them from our separate perspectives. It shapes up like this: the freshmen are coming from a successful high school experience. They expect to continue behaving in the same way they did in high school in order to succeed in college. This means they expected to:

1. Study hard even if they hated what they were studying, not because they believed it would be good for them or that others knew best, but simply on the grounds that this is what you have to do to succeed
2. Ask questions that made the professor think they were interested

so (a) they would be noticed or (b) they would clarify a
question that might arise in examinations

3. Stay away from professors' offices because (a) they might be too
busy and be annoyed if you bother them, or (b) you might let a
professor know how little you really understood his course
content

4. Try to find out as quickly as possible which courses would give a
good grade without much work

5. Meet people in each class who could support them in a number of
ways—for example, providing missed class notes after ab-
sences, explaining problems you don't understand, reducing
anxiety by admitting shared ignorance and fear

The list goes on, but the point of view clearly present is that the
freshmen gear themselves for a competitive struggle and in the beginning want as much of an edge over others as they can get. They know
they have already made it once before (in the high school game), but
they are not sure this game is played by the same rules. During these
orientation programs, therefore, they want to add as much as they can to
their repertoire of survival skills.

Parents see it in much the same way, but share some of the university
sentiments with which their children do not bother. They seem, somewhere deep down, to share the expectation of some university personnel
that students may gain some intrinsic joy from their college experiences. This would be in the form (the way they imagine it) of wise
messages or truths which the young people will clamp onto and thereby
take giant steps in the getting mature game. At the same time, many
parents expect university people to take some responsibility as surrogate
parents, aiding in the growing-up process and guarding the virginal
young minds against those corrupt forces rampant in the adult world.
With considerable support, one father finally risked stating his feelings:
he suggested we patrol the students' living quarters to guard against
drugs and members of the opposite sex who might have immoral sexual
designs on these children.

From our side of the fence we had to confide in the parents as well as
the freshmen that, yes, there was that element of fighting for survival.
Yes, we did separate out the wheat from the chaff and that the first year
was critical in that particular process. We offered what advice we could

regarding the best possible strategies for the ensuing survival-level competition. Then we spent an inordinate amount of time suggesting and discussing the many ways students could gain important under-standings of both themselves and the real world while attending college.

I think the shuck implicit in this kind of emphasis is in the fact that we digress from reality, and talk about how things should be, rather than how they are. To say that things are possible does not help much in an environment structured to make those possibilities remote. For reasons we all know well, it is not really possible to read, for example, both the books you would like to read and the ones you are requried to read in the same short quarter, when mid-terms, finals, and term papers all intervene and require much busy work.

In the final analysis, well-socialized kids, by the time they approach college age, know the difference between the shuck and the reality, and also expect to encounter both whenever they deal with institutions and persons who represent those institutions. I think the kids in the orienta-tion program knew, for example, that we were shucking when we talked about the many potential growth experiences and the freedom to make one's own choices and learn in one's own way. They knew what they had to do and they would do it. And I suppose, after all, that is really what we wanted all the time—if not, we would somehow try to bring the shuck into alignment with reality. But we wouldn't ever do that, of course, because then we would lose control over their behavior and God knows where that would lead.

CHAPTER EIGHT

The Learning Shuck

In the old style school, the kind with walls and seats lined in rows and adults standing at the head of a group of children, telling them what to do, learning can be described in two different ways. One way is to talk about what skills children learn, like reading or cooking; subject matter, such as history or geography; and manners, such as respecting authority and not digging your initials into desks. The other way is to talk about how we know children have learned. And this means thinking about the behaviors we accept as appropriate indicators of learning. In the earlier grades we look for skills and habits, and even though we know the difference between being able to spell and showing respect for the teachers's authority, it often turns out we confuse the two kinds of learning, at least in our final assessment of the learners. For some reason, the poor speller who had bad manners is a slow learner and the poor speller who has good manners is an underachiever.

I suppose one of the basic reasons I'm such a strong supporter of new forms of learning is that I was myself such a failure at the old forms; except for reading, which I could do well and early in life. Almost all other learning tasks found me, by the criteria most of my teachers used, at the bottom of the ladder. I couldn't spell, I couldn't make electric bells ring, I couldn't construct a bookcase in woodshop or shoot baskets in gym, or remember dates in history or capital cities in geography, and my math papers were usually both wrong and messy. In high school and college, I flunked both Latin and Spanish, and in graduate school I got the lowest score in the statistics course. So how did I get to be a college professor? I had such a good vocabulary and such a marvelously complex way of describing things, most of my professors thought I was very bright and overlooked most of my bad scores on objective and competency tests.

Anybody who has been a lifelong reader and uses lots of abstract words in very complex sentences can do it. I suspect the worst hypocrisy I ever perpetrated as a school teacher was during the years in which I graded kids in my English class on grammar and spelling and gave them low grades to signify that they hadn't learned anything. I even shared with the other teachers the notion that students who got F's on their report cards were poor learners. Now I believe you can't say how good a learner a child is until he tries to learn something he wants to learn. Unfortunately there is neither time nor a proper student-teacher ratio in schools to wait for that to happen.

We had a kid in my old junior high who was the worst learner in the school. He flunked everything all the time. His name was Manny. He was, on the average, about six inches shorter than the next smallest kid in everybody's class. We all liked him because he was so amusing, but he never passed a test or learned how to read. It somehow seems wrong to grade a kid on a social studies test who can't read, doesn't it? We assume it tells us something about his performance in social studies. But we do it all the time. We don't worry about it, though, because it doesn't hold him back. We promote everybody.

When most kids fail to "learn," they either get hostile, which distracts us from our responsibility to them, or they try harder, which persuades us we've been doing the right thing for them all along. When they seem not to care or want to withdraw, we assume they are just crazy. And once we define someone as crazy, especially if he isn't a discipline problem, we just treat him as if he were a little puppy dog, a mascot. Manny was our mascot. What I am sure of now, and what I suspected then, was that Manny's problem was that he had never learned the appropriate responses to not learning. That is, he was simply inadequately socialized.

Manny was the stereotype of the slow learner. He just didn't seem to be able to catch on to anything the teachers tried to teach him. I think by about the seventh grade everyone stopped expecting anything from him and let him do almost anything he liked since he was not particularly disruptive. He had long black hair that curled over his forehead like wire bangs. He seemed to bounce rather than walk, and he would pop up like a jack-in-the-box in places where students would neither be expected to go nor usually want to go. He would direct traffic in the halls at random times although he was not a hall monitor. He would appear among a group of teachers, below their line of vision and just be there, in on the conversation although not saying a word, not questioning the fact that he didn't belong.

Now the point I want to make here is that learning in school is learning responses more than anything else. Manny simply had not learned the correct responses to failure; he just didn't seem to care. Somewhere along the line we'd failed to teach him to care, so that when he didn't learn he would be suitably embarrassed, frustrated, hostile, or sick. He was in my seventh-grade English class and we were "learning grammar." Here were a bunch of kids who could hardly read a sentence, much less punctuate one, but the curriculum guide called for punctuation. Manny always copied out the sentences as he was expected to, and then proceeded to punctuate them. He put an upside down question mark here and there randomly, threw periods and commas in, and even dotted an I with an apostrophe. I watched with amusement and to my initial surprise saw his hand go up when I asked for someone to give me the answers.

He got out of his seat and came over to show me what I already knew was there. I said something like "Manny, you didn't get one right." He smiled and said "It's OK teach, don't worry about it. I didn't have anything else to do."

Manny was one of my unforgettables. Every school has at least one like him all the time. They are put there to remind us we are taking ourselves too seriously, and also to call our attention to the possibility that our learning games are total shucks.

Many students are being kept out of the public schools these days but, unfortunately, just long enough that when they return from their try at "free" schools, they will be unable to respond in ways which bring rewards from school personnel. I used the illustration of Manny, who in my day was an extreme exception. But these days there are bound to be thousands of unsocialized kids throughout the country running loose in public schools. Perhaps I should have said "walking," since children are always warned in a loud, authoritative voice: "No running in the halls!"

Manny could find no way, no need, to relate the conventions of schooling to himself. George, on the other hand, was so well socialized that he made it difficult for himself to stay in a situation where he might have learned at least those things other high school students were learning, like how to survive in high school and beyond. The problem with George was that he brought with him the values he had learned in elementary school, and didn't pick up enough of the new stuff about how to shuck your way through everything.

In the end, George dropped out of school and went to work in a shoe store as a stock boy. He just got tired of struggling with school. For some reason, though, George brought me his last English essay assignment almost two weeks after he had dropped out. He never showed up to see what I thought of it, so it wasn't for my approval. Probably he felt he owed me the paper since the relationship we had developed went beyond what he did to be in my class. I want to quote just the last part of his paper, which is pertinent to our concern with learning.

I had a day off work last week so I went back to school. I was just hanging around by the fence and some kid I didn't know came out and told me I was not allowed to be hanging out by the fence. If I didn't leave he would call the cops to make me leave. The thing that came to my mind is why would they want to keep anybody out? They must think they have something very valuable in there or they wouldn't want to guard it. Most kids I know wanted to get out and here they were keeping me from coming in.

On the other hand I was trying to think what it was that made me want to be there. Since I really didn't get much out of being there in the first place. I mean, I didn't learn anything that I can think of. Everything I know now I kind of knew before I went there. Maybe I know a couple more words and can spell a few I couldn't spell before and I guess I remember something about World War I that I didn't know before, like the names of General Koch and General Pershing. But that doesn't seem like much for two and a half years of a person's time.

I guess when it comes down to it I really can't blame anybody but myself for the things I didn't learn. I never really took school very seriously. I mean I never fell in love with any subject like history or English or anything. The main thing I was interested in was girls and just getting by. I never learned much about girls either, but I guess school isn't the place for that although I don't know what place is.

There was one thing about girls I did learn now that I think of it. It's that most girls are looking for a guy with the right kind of background, who takes the right courses and is in the right curriculum. And that a girl who loves a guy like that hasn't any time for anybody else. There were a lot of girls that talked to me when I was in college prep, but as soon as I was shifted to vocational the same girls wouldn't even say hello. When I was sitting on the vice-principal's bench they would walk by and look right through me like they couldn't imagine knowing anybody who would be in my situation.

One of these girls was Lilly Middleman the cheerleader who was dating a guy by the name of Peter Wasserman. We were all in college prep together and Lilly and I would talk a lot in classes and around the school but outside she spent all her time with Pete. She used to tell me she enjoyed talking with me because I was very intelligent and could understand where she was at and things like that which Pete couldn't. She said Pete was only interested because she was in love with him. When I got transferred to Mr. Green's homeroom, she stopped talking to me completely. What I learned from this was that intelligence and understanding somebody doesn't count for a whole lot when love is involved.

Talking about Pete and Lilly reminds me of a couple of other things I learned while I was at Cuney High. That first year we were in the same English class with Mr. Moody, the three of us were, and both Pete and Lilly were doing very poor and we had this book report that was going to count a lot. Anyhow, Pete never read anything but car magazines and sports, and Lilly read some books but never understood them. I usually had read a couple of extra books and could write a pretty good report so I did it for both of them. (I hope this can be kept confidential since I wouldn't want to interfere with their college plans.) Then when we all got back our grades they got B's and I got a C. What I figured out from that is who you are counts more than what you do. I know that as little as I ever learned there Pete learned a lot less and Lilly probably nothing at all but they're going to college and I'm not. Pete's father made the difference. He was an important man in something and he would come around a lot and talk to the teachers and got him tutors and all and pulled him through. It shows you that influence counts.

It keeps coming to me new things I remember I learned, now that I'm writing about it. I guess I'm learning something right now by doing this, that if somebody sat me down and gave me a test in school and just asked me to write everything I learned in high school I wouldn't even be able to fill up a page. But doing it this way where it doesn't count for anything a lot of things come to mind. For example, I was just thinking that one of the most important things I learned was that what a kid did wasn't nearly as important as how he did it. If I had had really good handwriting I know my grades would have been better. Lilly had excellent handwriting and even though she didn't say anything on her papers she always did all right.

Samuel Johnson the class president was another one who did fine because he sounded good and looked good. He always dressed fine and said good things about the school and got elected to lots of things so he was almost never in class but he got better grades in those classes that he wasn't in than I did and I went every day. So that's another thing, the way you look counts a lot. There wasn't a single person in any school that I ever went to who was elected for anything that wasn't pretty good looking. And they all did fine in their grades too. I can't believe that good looks and intelligence go together but that's what it seems like if you go by school grades.

One of the things I learned best was how to make up excuses adults would buy. Like the time I was trying to get back into college prep, for a while I got some support from a couple of teachers when I dropped the expression "broken home." Even Mr. Moody seemed to understand why I wasn't doing too well in English when I mentioned about my father leaving when I was about ten. I used that lots of times in different situations, whenever I could get it in naturally, and teachers seemed to change in the attitude and act like

they were really concerned and understood why things weren't going
well.

I also learned how to cheat without getting caught. How to figure
out teachers in terms of what bullshit they go for. How to look like
you're interested when you're falling asleep in a class. Those kind of
things. So why am I a dropout? I'm not sure. I guess I just didn't
learn all those things well enough. I didn't become an expert.

If George had ever wanted a recommendation to college I would have
been happy to write one for him, but I don't know where he is anymore
and he's probably past the age of believing school is the answer to
anything.

What kids are forced to learn in school is how to survive, how to
compete against their classmates for standard prizes and rewards. They
learn three basic strategies: do good, look good, and if you can't do
either, pull everybody else down so you show up better.

The first group is the do-goods. This is the student who learns what
his or her teacher expects in the way of performance and spends all the
time working on it. If the teacher expects two book reports, they do two
and if he will accept another for extra credit, they'll do that one too.
They do all their math homework at home and all their classwork in
class. If you watch them they look like they're really caught up in their
work, even interested, but if you ask them they'll tell you "no," it's
just something they have to do. They have learned teachers like indus-
triousness and will reward it, even in the absence of any apparent
learning. By the time they get to high school and college we see them as
grade getters and that is what their entire learning experience has been.
Unfortunately, even pathetically, I have seen the faces of many of these
grades getters when they experience for the first time the awareness that
they have blown it. I have often spoken to them as college seniors,
ready to walk off the campus for the last time, and at the same moment
realizing for the first time that all they have to show for all those years of
grade getting is a degree. I even smile sadistically when I see them
realize the degree is not worth very much these days.

Some of them, though not many, are able to grasp the full
significance of those untold hours of study and its monumental
irrelevance to anything they really know to be important. These kids,

after the first agonizing period of self-disgust, then parent and teacher disgust, finally come round to a reappraisal and a new start, at which point schooling becomes a whole new concept.

Understanding this too early in one's career can be a personal disaster. One of the things I told my orientation freshmen was that they had to be careful not to discover any significance or importance in their lives prior to becoming seniors, when they could coast out on their laurels. I said this in jest, of course, but many of the freshmen, and, on the average they seemed to be more aware than our seniors, understood the seriousness of the issue in their own terms. One little girl looked up at me from her double lotus position on the floor and said, "Professor, I can play the game as good as I have to but I can also keep up with me and if you and the other professors intend to stop me from doing that you've got another think coming."

"How are you going to stop us from forcing you to play the grade-getter game?" I asked with a superior smile.

"Easy," she said. "Just choose not to."

The thing that shook up my system at that moment was the fact that a mere college freshman understood something that it took me about 35 years just to have a hint of, that you can choose not to play the game.

I have not yet been able to discover where some of these freshmen learned about the possibility of alternatives. I'm afraid, from some of the comments they have made, it has at least something to do with various illegal behaviors in which they engage. I won't deal with these here because I have no desire to encourage illegal behavior. But I am very willing to suggest that some kind of learning process appears to go on in the hallucinogenic experience, and that this appears to bear some relationship to turning away from grade getting. I have not yet explored the dynamics, but I intend to do so.

The second type of learning involves those who learn the strategies of looking good. In college we have the front rowers, who sit up straight and look as if they are deeply involved in what you're saying. They ask questions at regular intervals. Then, when they get C's on their exams and come in to tell you they hadn't slept all night and their mother just had a tumor removed, you're more inclined to believe the "bad day" excuse because they look so alert in class.

Now take it down about 13 or 14 years to a bunch of first or second graders sitting in rows. The teacher asks a question about something or other and 30 little hands shoot up. You can count on one hand the number of them who have the right answer.

I've watched these first graders try to look good and I never have figured out where they got the particular mentality that says raise your hand even if you don't know the answer. It's better to chance not being called on than not raise your hand. After all, only one kid can be called on at a time. It's kind of an American roulette that kids learn to play very early. Looking good does involve some risks, though, and every once in a while you end up looking bad trying to look good.

Some kids learn how to look good about looking bad, like one little kid I knew in my junior high school. He made it through school by looking good when he was caught being bad. He would violate every rule in the book, like sneaking in the lunch line, copying everything from everybody else, smoking in the bathroom. And every time you would catch him at something, you'd find yourself involved in his little game. It was always so amusing, you'd look forward to catching him. His act was so polite and respectful, and his excuses so preposterous that you had to credit him for brightening up your day.

Once I caught him smoking in the boys' bathroom. Here he was, caught red-handed. The cigarette was smoking away, right between his fingers. "All right, Linzey," I said, "you've had it this time." He didn't even whirl around or attempt to fling the butt into the john.

"I beg your pardon," he said, with poise.

"You've had it now," I repeated. "Smoking's a suspension violation."

"Smoking?" he said with surprise. "SMOKING?"

"Smoking, Linzey. There's a cigarette burning between your index and third fingers."

"Well," he said, "that's really true. I am holding a cigarette, but I'm not smoking."

"What are you getting at?" I asked.

"Well, I've got my shoes on my feet but I'm not walking."

I granted it was good thinking, but I couldn't let it go. There were too many kids watching me and I had to look good too. Otherwise they would all pull the same line on me and my bathroom duty had another week to go.

"Come on Linzey," I said, "I've got you for holding, then."

"But I wasn't holding for me," he said, very seriously. "This fellow comes up to me and says hold this, I've got to take a leak and I see he's much bigger than me and I can't refuse or tell him to hold it himself."

"Why not?"

"Well, you don't want to get pee on a good butt."

Linzey always had style. He makes films now with other people's money and I'm sure he's doing well. I'm sure he makes pornographic movies with a lot of class and is bound to get rich at it. I've never seen any of his movies, but I'm sure they look good.

Looking good in school is often a matter of getting called on so you can show off whatever stuff you know. Jules Henry, the anthropologist who writes about schools, tells the story of the time he visited a music class in an elementary school. The teacher was playing the piano and the kids had their music books open in front of them and everything was going on well until about the last 16 bars of the song, when suddenly all singing voices were obscured by a hugh rustling of paper. It took a couple of songs before Henry figured out what was going on. It turned out that the way the songs were selected was that the teacher let the kids pick them and called on someone to choose the next song. Naturally, just before the end of each piece, everybody was looking for another song to choose so they could be the one called upon by the teacher.

Some students have the hand-raising gambit down to an art. What you do is wait until the very last moment, the split second before the teacher opens her mouth to call on someone else, when you're sure she has her mind made up and a name other than yours is about to be called. Up goes your hand to answer the question and you haven't the foggiest notion what the answer could be. If the kid she calls on misses the answer and she then calls on you, you can always say you were thinking the same thing as the last student. If she calls on somebody else, you play your game again.

The children who are good at looking good are usually the ones who psych out the teacher to find out what his special interests are and then pretend to have the same interest. I had one teacher in high school who loved chess, so I bought a little set and kept it on my desk. Every once in a while, before class, a friend and I would pretend to be playing. The teacher came up to us and showed us a couple of strategies and took the first 20 minutes of class to demonstrate. Nobody cared even if they didn't know anything about chess because grammar was on the schedule. Anyway, my friend and I both found our grades improving, especially the grades on our compositions.

I also remember a history teacher from high school who hated Roosevelt as much as most people loved him. The most certain way to get an A in history was to write some critical comment about Roosevelt on a test question, even if it didn't fit in. Kids who are good at looking good can always find a way to get almost anything down on a test. They have a way of rephrasing almost any test question to allow them to tell what they know rather than try to give the teacher the correct answer. If we were studying about the Louisianna purchase and answering a question like "Why did Jefferson want the territory?" I would come up with something like:

> Jefferson wanted the land for the people so they could be individual-ists and go out and make a place for themselves. It was the kind of thing a great president like Jefferson would have wanted, not like Roosevelt who took everything away from the people and gave it to the government.

That kind of statement would have clearly indicated to the teacher that I was a good student. Otherwise, how could I have had such insight about Roosevelt and made the connection from that all the way back to Jefferson?

Looking good frequently means an appeal to the ego of the evaluator. "If he comes up with the same conclusion I have, then he must be a bright person, since this is the way I figured it out and of course my intelligence isn't in question."

Little children are funny, the way they exaggerate all their looking good. I've seen first-grade classes in which the kids look like they are about to snap because they are all standing and/or sitting so straight and proper. And speaking in class becomes a matter of recitation rather than saying what's on your mind. By the time they all grow up and go to high school or college, the edge is off and strategies for looking good just roll off their fingers. They've learned the game.

That, I believe, is what they have learned best in their years in school—the game of looking good; and if you can't look good, then make sure the other guy doesn't either, which is our next learning category. The pulley strategy is something kids learn very early in the school battle. It's a way of uplifting yourself by pushing others down, a common practice in most areas of social life. In school it takes a number of specific forms: first and earliest it is the tattle. Later on in life this is referred to as the FINK.

In the name of protecting the values, rather than the self, little children rush to the teacher to tell on their classmates. "Johnny opened his milk before you said to," or "Tommy is copying from my paper," or "Billy didn't wash his hands after painting." Usually the tattle game among really young ones consists of girls trying to make boys look bad. I must agree that at that age, and by classical school standards, boys *are* bad compared with girls. And the girls are quick to bring the proof to the teacher's attention. Later on, boys get even by convincing girls it isn't feminine to know much. Sometimes they take the "what man would want a wife who knows more than he does?" route, and in the long run get back much more than what they were subjected to in the early years.

Teachers frequently encourage tattling on the grounds that the values thus protected are more important than the destruction of character resulting from students seeing their classmates as legitimate game in open season. As a substitute teacher working on my graduate degree, I had assignments in several elementary schools. In almost every class at least one of two sweet little girls would come up to me before class and give me a big welcome; afterward they always gave me a list of the students I should keep my eye on during the day.

Teaching in high school, I knew kids who always had two algebra homework papers prepared, one with the right answers for the teacher and one with wrong answers for the kids who didn't do their homework and wanted to borrow. It can get that bad. In every high school which I ever studied, attended, or taught, I found cliques of kids who would support each other and conspire to wash out those who were not in the clique. These kids were always in conversation with the teacher and often got hints about the content of upcoming tests. This information they would only share with their own.

Another pulley technique teachers encourage is the one where the teacher calls on some kid for an answer and the second he flounders, all the kids who know the answer start flapping their arms and going "oooh oooh" as they stretch their hands into the teacher's face. Then all the first kid can think of is all the others he sees and hears who know what he can't figure out. It's one thing not to know, but it's quite another to be the victim of those who do. I remember well how it felt to be the victim. We all know kids are cruel and insensitive, but it takes adults to organize their lives in such a way that they can utilize these qualities effectively against each other.

When I was a camp counselor we had a rule that if a little kid wet his bed he would not be allowed to go swimming for two days and would get on the bad side of the counselor. One little five year old would get up in the middle of the night and pee on other kids' beds. After four or five kids, who swore they didn't do it were punished, we got suspicious and began to watch more carefully. It wasn't long before we caught the little one engaged in his dirty work. When we asked him why he did it he said he wanted to get kids he didn't like in trouble. The dangerous thing about this attitude is that some people, like this kid, don't like anyone. The whole pulley strategy is usually well developed in children by the age of five and everything after that age is just a matter of subtle refinement, especially for people who don't like anybody.

Since so many college students have academic ambitions beyond what they perceive to be their talents, they often blatantly protect the sanctity of what they do know so the others won't do better on tests. Professors and teachers encourage this private property version of knowledge by grading on the curve, a practice one of my colleagues has publicly labeled "bell-shaped bullshit." In some high schools I've seen two opposite adaptations to this phenomena. In nonacademic high schools, where few students intend to go to college, they have a "rate buster" norm which tells students they'll be in trouble with their peers if they do too well. In the suburban high schools the opposite is the case. The rate buster norm doesn't get going even though some kids get wiped out trying to keep up with the future doctors and engineers.

I've spoken to a lot of college kids about this phenomenon. It has interested me for a long time. Many tell me that in study sessions, even with their friends, they keep some of the stuff they know to themselves and thus keep the edge on everybody else. Each of them thinks he's the only person who is holding back; just picture a study session in which everybody holds back. Fortunately they never go over their exams together or they would catch on to each other. Since learning something after a test is irrelevant, it is unlikely this will ever be revealed.

The learning shuck covers a wide range of student-teacher behaviors, but the one I think the most obvious on the side of the teachers is that many define learning in terms of what they teach. A couple of years back I observed a teacher classically engaged in this particular egocentric shuck.

Miss Smith was teaching a history class on the subject of the Tudor kings of England. Jack, a poor student, had been uninvolved and distracted most of the semester, but Miss Smith had encouraged him to bring his grade up by working for extra credit. This particular day Miss Smith asked the class if anybody had done a report on Henry the VIII and Jack, to my surprise and hers, raised his hand. Jack read from his paper for a few minutes and then was interrupted by Miss Smith:

"For crying out loud, Jack, you've got the wrong Henry."

"The wrong Henry?" he responded, in mild shock.

"Yes, you're talking about the seventh and you were supposed to do something about the eighth."

The obvious point of this little horror story is that Jack was learning something about English history, which was not his style in the first place, and he was put down because he was not learning what the teacher was teaching. In school terms, you'd say he wasn't learning at all since, if Miss Smith had given a test on Henry the VIII, Jack would have gotten a zero. It probably all came about because Jack couldn't differentiate one roman numeral from another.

Having described what children actually learn in school—how to shuck, compete, survive—we now come to a conception of what teachers and even higher educators define as learning. Learning is performance. More specifically, it is performance as defined and measured by the teacher. The categories in which this learning can be evaluated can be broken down into such performance areas as homework, classwork-written, classwork-verbal, tests, and projects. The standard approach to this in both lower and higher schooling is that the teacher has a view of what it is he is trying to teach and consequently defines learning in those terms. That is, has the student learned what I am teaching? The teacher devises criteria for measuring what he is teaching; performance on those criteria is what learning is. Nothing else qualifies, and nothing could be simpler. Except for a few minor difficulties, for example:

1. Does teacher really know what he is teaching?
2. Does the teacher know how to evaluate what is learned?

3. Can learning be said to have occurred if it doesn't come out in performance?
4. Can the thing to be learned ever "make sense" years later under another very different set of life experiences?
5. Is it possible that students could have used the teaching as a takeoff for other learnings unrelated to the teacher's criteria?
6. What score is the learning cutoff—50 percent, 72 percent, 84 percent?
7. How deep an understanding does learning require?
8. How do you measure depth of understanding ?

In the junior high where I taught, the average student couldn't read very well, but that didn't stop us from teaching everything out of books. At the same time all of our tests were taken from the books the students could barely read, and most of the kids failed most of the time. I had a class of "slow learners" in social studies and we were studying American imperialism, under some other label. We were talking about how we developed the Panama Canal and I told them it took many months of toil and struggle and sickness to dig it through from ocean to ocean. Then I pulled down the map and pointed to Panama and they all looked at each other and started to smile.

"Shoot, teach," came the first reply, "them sure were some lazy workers takin' all that time to dig through that little sliver."

I laughed and told them the little sliver was a lot of miles of very hard earth to work through.

"Yea," said another, "I'm hip to them stories. A man who's diggin' has got to tell you it's a hard job, otherwise he's got to work harder."

It occurred to me at that moment they were relating my classroom talk to their own lives, as if anything else were possible. I urged them to believe me, the little sliver was a lot of miles and was a hard job. I had run up against their conception of how workers have to lie to the boss and their inability to grasp the notion of scale size and proportion. If I could have flown them there, to Panama, they might have learned something, but all my talk could accomplish was an "uh huh," or two. I think they believed me but that doesn't mean anything. They didn't learn, they were just convinced by my credibility. If I asked them on a test about the size of Panama I probably would have gotten a correct answer, but I know that isn't learning.

Lessons don't always bring the understandings teachers expect; you can't always get at the real learnings. Teachers usually classify a child as a good learner if he gives the teacher the performance for which he or she is looking. Put that way, learning is simply a label for meeting the teacher's specific expectations. When you think about it, you have to admit this is a very narrow conception of learning.

My colleagues who study learning are a little bit like clergy who study God. First they decide what it is, then they go about studying it. When I tell them we don't know very much about learning, they go on and cite hundreds of learning studies they either know of or have themselves done. Then I say I doubt if that's learning, and that if their conception of learning is incorrect, then they don't know anything about learning. On the other hand, the fact that they get full professorships for all those studies proves the institution believes them, even if I don't. If the institutions doubted the credibility of what they call learning, they wouldn't be promoted for all those learning studies.

It's a vicious cycle. Look at it this way. I do a learning study and it gets published. That means my professional colleagues accept my version of learning. Now how am I ever going to change my conception of learning when everybody rewards me for the one I've got? In this way, institutionalized learning, particularly in higher education, encourages the status quo and discourages innovation. This is not a new criticism; anyone who has ever tried to change a time-honored conception of something knows his major enemies are institutional types who have a vested interest in maintaining the status quo.

I wouldn't make much of an argument if it were only a matter of the theory and the research activities of college professors, but unfortunately this state of affairs has serious direct and indirect effects on schools and millions of kids. Primarily, it leads to the development of tests which they claim measure learning. The tests do not measure learning, however, they simply define what they do measure *as* learning. Teachers then teach to tests, since they want their classes to look good. High school students study what they know is going to be on college entrance board exams and that too defines learning. Teachers in Los Angeles and many other cities must take tests to become teachers, and these also define a specific version of learning.

Another major result of the vicious cycle in California is that teachers are required to learn to write things called behavioral objectives.

Whether officially sanctioned or not, the behaviorist model of education is relatively entrenched in education in this country, and the criteria for learning thereby implanted in the values of teachers and through them in the heads of children, is that kids have to *do something*. Behavioral means "observable." We have to see it. If we can't see it, it doesn't exist. Even the people who create these objectives know things can exist which we can't observe. But the problem there is that the existence of something we can't observe becomes defined as irrelevant, not because it doesn't exist but because we can't get at it.

That's all right for scientists, but should educators accept the same value? The comparison between scientists and educators as I'm making it here is this: if I'm a psychologist looking at human behavior, I can work down any path I choose as long as we have reached a stage of development where I can measure what I study. If I believe in anything as mystical and unmeasurable as sources for human motivation, I'd better keep this belief to myself. Otherwise I might get criticized or fired for being nonscientific. As a scientist, I accept the rules for scientific inquiry. If I don't, then I'm something other than a scientist. Now educators who study learning seem to think the same criteria applies to them, as if they were scientists (which they may be, for all I care). When, however, what they do to children is based upon a very limited and probably incorrect assessment of what teaching is and what learning is, then I feel I have to make the argument.

Very simply, it goes something like this: When we define learning as something that can be measured by some performance, some observable behavior, we limit the child to that outcome and totally ignore not only what he might have learned while we pushed him toward our objectives, but what he might have learned if we hadn't had the objectives for him in the first place.

The predictable outcome of this shuck is that we do all sorts of things to kids in terms of these performances, including washing them out of school when they can't perform. It's one thing to impose an unreality on a kid, and it's another to punish him because he refuses to buy our unreality and clings to his own.

An example of an objective is "The child will read three pages in ten minutes from a fourth-grade reader." If, after a series of attempts to get the kid to do this, we find he cannot, we automatically conclude he has not yet learned. What we mean is he has not yet learned to do this task.

It would still all be well and good if we would just let it go at that. Unfortunately what has taken hold of schooling is not the specific reference of the single task, like reading, but the generalized form of education that emerges from the use of objectives. So he can't read three pages in ten minutes from a fourth-grade reader—fine, for score keepers. But now what becomes of the child who has the low score at the time we take the count? If we had only waited until he was ready, he wouldn't have the low score, and therefore his sign, which educators seem to know what to do with.

Learning, as I see it, is an experience no one can precisely tap, since only the learner has it. Why can't we just let that be, rather than creating standards in the objective world he must struggle to meet?

Some of my colleagues think it would be immoral and irresponsible not to keep check on whether or not our teaching methods are working. To me, immorality becomes an issue only when we start trying to see if our methods work so we won't be immoral. It's a little bit like beating a kid to see how much pain he can take before you write a specific, individualized beating program for him. If beating isn't a good idea in the first place, then why build a whole tried and tested methodology around it?

The alternative to the learning shuck is first to understand that what students learn is hardly confined to academic matters. Second, we must then figure out what useful informalities might be introduced so students would learn how to deal with them. For example, suppose we give students an hour a day of free time, with no restrictions. They will probably learn how to use leisure time which, in an automated society, might be useful. Third, since students learn how to please us teachers, we have to make it more difficult for them, since we don't want to call learning the advice they get from others who have gone before. Why don't we randomize our standards and expectations, changing them so often that the student can never be sure of what he has to do to make us happy? At that point, since he can't figure out how to please us he might try to please himself, which I think would be productive. Finally we would force kids to construct their own evaluation schemes and evaluate themselves. Once we put them to work doing that then, since they want to do well, they will devise criteria for performance based upon what they think they can do well, or at least upon what they are interested in. This saves teachers the effort of constructing their own criteria and at the same time avoids the criticism of the "relevent" mongers that we are measuring what we want and not what students want.

Whether or not one agrees with the above strategy it must be apparent that an alternative to the learning shuck requires a reconstruction of all those structures which I have outlined in Chapter Ten. In constructing a new system of education the learning shuck is more important as a point of initial attack than any other—because every activity and interaction involves learning. When you get to Chapter Ten I hope you will have at least some reconstruction possiblities in the back of your mind.

I don't know one teacher who doesn't have some sense as to whether or not kids are having a good experience. They still use their intuition better than they use evaluation techniques. But at this point our curriculum guides are forcing all kids to be stuffed into learning packages with specific objectives at the end. That makes schooling our version of learning, and we have to take the blame for the monumental failure public education has become, partly as a result of this, in our time. Of course we can always shuck it off onto the teachers on the grounds that they can't follow our instructions. But I think they follow very well. Most kids know they have to perform and know the specific forms this performance must take. When we discover after all, that we have made our children into Performance Objects, perhaps we will consider there are other things or people or beings they might be.

CHAPTER NINE

The Free School Shuck

On the left, or "far out" from the mainstream of conventional shuck schooling is an educational experience affectionately referred to as the "free school." Such schools are not free in the sense of not charging money. Although some don't charge tuition, free schools usually cost more than public or parochial schools. But that's no shuck. If you leave the mainstream of any culture, or the system, you have to be prepared to pay the price of doing so. Parents who agree to rebel are usually very aware of at least the financial consequences of their deviation. Free schools may well be an improvement over the rigidly moralistic and profession-oriented closed classroom style of the public school. Yet they also operated upon a number of assumptions which, as I see them, are as much a shuck as anything that the public schools can come up with.

The major shuck assumption of the free school is that "anybody can be a teacher." This means, regardless of age, training, experience, or knowledge, anyone can teach a child something, which is probably true, as far as it goes. The implications, however, go much further.

They indicate that any housewife, carpenter, or engineer can just stop what he or she is doing, move to an average classroom, replace an average teacher, and do just as well. This is also probably true. But the shuck occurs when we take it one step further and say that, since this is all true, then we might as well start our own school and teach our own kids: we can do it as well as anybody.

That is a shuck. It makes it possible for anybody who feels like it to become a teacher. It totally ignores the possibility that maybe there is such a thing as a real teacher, and that perhaps there are people around who have certain skills other people don't have. And if this isn't so, then maybe it is possible to train persons to do something that an average housewife can't do, given some thought and effort, and maybe even training.

Housewives and engineers, working vacations and part time, can open free schools only because they conveniently buy the notion that kids have to develop their own learning in their own way and that it's generally a good idea, instead of giving kids something to learn, simply to call learning whatever it is they do. Now, if whatever kids do is learning, granted they're doing something, then why do we need anything more than baby sitters to watch over them and make sure they don't hurt each other? This too would be learning, wouldn't it? I mean, how do we learn not to fight unless we fight and don't like it?

But the main problem with nonteacher teachers is that they begin to act exactly like teachers. Fully and painfully recognizing that they don't have the faintest idea how to teach anybody anything, their insecurity leads them to pounce upon the first idea that comes along. I've seen public school teachers eagerly embrace systems and methods of instruction filtered down through the administration. And I've seen insecure, nonteacher teachers put kids through absolute hoops to carry out a so-called teaching idea.

One such teacher studied Gestalt psychology with Fritz Pearls. (What studied means in the counterculture is two weekend workshops and an hour together in the mineral baths.) Her idea was to put the kids in a big circle with one in the middle and have him act out his dreams and fantasies and change seats every time the role changed in his dreams. It seemed like fun and every kid wanted to do it and they started competing with each other to get the chance. But in order to get a chance you had to have a dream ready. And after a while it became evident, even to the seven-year-olds, that the teacher liked juicy, good dreams best because they gave her something "to work with." So the kids started making up dreams you couldn't imagine. Then, since they still had remnants of creative competition to work out, they began to accuse each of other of making up their dreams, which they all did do, of course. If only the teacher had been loose enough to drop the therapy and admit to fantasy games, for whatever they were worth—although I doubt she would have figured out a use for them—at least the competition would have ended.

Another teacher I observed heard from some encounter group leader she was working with about the value of avoiding questions. "Questions put people on the defensive," she said. Thus the rule formed: all we need to do in the nonteacher teacher role is give people feedback on what they are saying. It goes like this: A kid comes up to the nonteacher teacher and says, "I want to use Mary's green crayon."

The teacher answers: "Oh, you want to use the crayon."

Kid: "Yes, the crayon. Mary has it."

Teacher: "I see, Mary has it and you don't."

Kid: "Yes, and she won't let me have it."

Teacher: "Ah, I see, she's keeping it from you."

Kid: "Yes."

Teacher: "I see, she has it and you don't."

Kid (starting to cry in frustration): "Make her let me have it."

Teacher: "Oh, now I see, you would like me to ask Mary to let you use the crayon."

Kid: "Yes, make her do it."

Teacher: "Well then, let's have Mary over here and discuss the problem, Mary!" (Calls)

Mary: "Yes."

Teacher: "Mary, Jane has something to say to you."

Jane: "I need the green crayon."

Mary: "OK. I'm finished with it now, you can have it."

Teacher: "See how easy things can be worked out?"

Another similar assumption free school people make is that you can't teach anybody anything. They don't mean things like sewing and typing and reading, but the important things, like understanding life. Therefore they are going to provide children with the freedom to understand life.

If you just let children be, they will come to that glorious moment when truth makes itself known. This too is usually a shuck. Since we don't know what to do with kids and since we can't really teach them anything significant anyhow, we'll just provide them with an environment and they can try to explore their oneness with the universe. If they really believed that it were that simple to learn, it would seem to be more reasonable to me that they recommend that parents keep their kids at home. But since they know parents need to send their kids somewhere to get them out of the house and use some of that excess energy, the free school might as well pick up the slack. At least it's better being free than in prison.

I've looked in on free schools. I usually see kids wandering around aimlessly until some "facilitator" can't take it any longer and calls the "group" together to discuss what it is they should be doing with their time. This gets us into the next assumption. Children will be able to direct their own learning, "with a little help from their friends." I have waited, I have watched. I have seen a group of kids so hung up in their inability to make a decision that the first suggestion offered by the facilitator was jumped on like a loin of beef by a hungry lion. It has always amused me that such free kids should always end up choosing to study the things the facilitator knows best, like potting or macrame or playing the guitar. How come, I ask? Are these natural choices of free children? Would my children get into all of those things if they were free to choose? Why doesn't anybody choose arithmetic or spelling? I think the answer is obvious. In the same way that old or slave schools want to make kids into engineers and file clerks, new schools want to make them into potters, beaders, or folk singers. One is certainly as good as the other, but is that freedom to direct their own learning? A shuck.

Another assumption of free schoolers is that school should be a democracy: one man, one vote. I don't want to appear to be downgrading democracy, because I do believe in it in principle, and I think the fact that free schools consider democracy as an ideal is beautiful. I just think the democracy shuck is a matter of spreading the responsibility for ignorance around because nobody wants to take full charge for decision making or any meaningful doing. If you really want to observe a paralyzed faculty, go observe a free school for a few days. I watched a teacher make a decision for the group in a meeting and he almost tore his own tongue out after he realized what he'd done. It went like this.

A teacher: "Does anybody have a suggestion about what we should do about Donnie breaking Mary's sculpture?"

A kid: "How about making him stand in the library facing the books, but he can't read any of them."

Mary: "That won't bring my sculpture back."

Teacher: "Don't you think that's what your old public school teacher would have done?"

Same kid: "Sure, but it works."

Donnie: "Well, I was really mad at Mary."

Teacher: "Perhaps we should deal with the anger now. How does the group feel?"

Donnie: "Sure."

Mary: "No. Punish."

Bad teacher: "We decided to deal with the issue of punishment and I would like to see us at least complete that task."

Good teacher: "John, really. Don't you think the group has the right to evolve in its own direction?"

Bad teacher: "Of course." (Head down) "How could I . . . I mean . . . I was just so frustrated. We've been here so long- , . . . but I should have known better."

The discussion went on interminably and no decision was ever reached on either Donnie's anger or Donnie's punishment. After that little scenario, they got into a debate about how a group should evolve and whether or not it was important to finish something once started. Most of the kids looked very bewildered but the staff enjoyed the discussion immensely. They were getting paid for it. And after the group was disbanded, I heard one of the staff say to a visiting mother, "That was one of the most meaningful experiences the group has had."

Democracy becomes a shuck when we emphasize the struggle to evolve a process over the struggle to get kids involved in learning. I am not suggesting that the democratic process may not provide important learning experiences: I am only saying there are times when the process itself appears to be more important than the welfare of the members. "God damn it, we are going to do this democratically if I have to force you."

The truth of the matter is most kids don't really worry about who makes the decisions as long as they end up doing something that turns them on. I've seen kids spend anguishing hours being forced to democratically evolve a program when all they want is to be doing something. One teacher said something like, "No, Johnny, you can't go work on your tree house until the group decides what it wants to do." By the time they'd decided what to do, they had to hold their group project over until the next day because it was already too late to start anything.

Another assumption of the free school consciousness is that children are beautiful, aware, sensitive beings and are more humane than adults, and that, therefore, we must look to them for clues to our direction: "A little child shall lead them." I think these adults shuck it on about the beauty of children as a way of comparing our inadequate selves with what we might have been. And this faith in the natural goodness of children is, indeed, reasonable. I too affirm the value of children. I believe in them too. But this is one area in which it is very necessary for counter culturists to get some perspective. My point is that children do have certain qualities adults *should* regret losing, chief among them being openness and honesty and a lack of the debilitating self-consciousness that allows them to look bad or awkward and not be destroyed. And I do think we should celebrate life and humanness wherever we find it. Yet counter to the beliefs of free school people, I think we find what we like to call humaness more in adults than in children. Kids for the most part are insensitive to the feelings of their peers, are highly egocentric and self-serving, and treat adults, when they can, as relatively worthless creatures, which some may be. For the most part, I find children lack empathy. It is very difficult for them to sacrifice their own hedonistic needs for the benefit of a suffering adult.

I am leading up to another notion: we can discover our own beautiful models in adults who have suffered and grown; why not expose these to the children as portraits of leadership, insofar as a model becomes a leader? These models are teachers, perhaps the best we have, and it may be time we stopped worshiping the wisdom of children (which they, in fact, lack), and concentrate on their human worth and need for models of growth. This recommendation carries over into the area of group democracy as well. Leaders should have the courage to lead and the wisdom to know that children cannot lead themselves. This does not mean children should ever be required to do anything except respect another's well being. It does mean that leadership can be conceived of as attracting participation, not coercing it.

Another assumption of free school types is the idea that "children need to get their feelings out.'' The thing that most characterizes a free school environment is a bunch of children and adults sitting around either yelling at each other or being prodded to express their feelings. A typical session in the junior-senior high age group, without characters, goes like this:

"Johnny, I know you must be mad at Nancy for walking away from you."

"No, I'm not. Honest. I feel alright."

"I know if somebody I was speaking to turned and walked away I would be very hurt and angry."

"Yea, but you're not me."

"But I have feelings like you."

"I didn't walk away like you said. I said excuse me and had to go to the bathroom."

"Come on, Nancy. Don't clean it up. If you felt like walking away from Johnny, he's going to have to face it and deal with it. We can't protect each other from the real world, now can we?"

"Now, come on, Claude, how come you're trying to put your own anger out on Johnny? Obviously you have some feelings about Nancy that you're not sharing with us."

"Nancy? Who, me? Nancy, she's alright. No, I think it's OK if she walks away. I'm not putting her down."

"I didn't walk away."

"Why are you so hostile to Johnny, Nancy? We might as well get that out in the open."

"Bullshit. I'm not hostile."

"Of course you are, you sound it."

"I'm just hostile at all this crap going down here."

"Don't slough it off on us, baby. It's your hangup."

The End.

After the session the "facilitator" took a bunch of big pillows out of a closet and started a pillow fight so all the anger not dealt with in the session could be filtered off by smashing pillows against everybody else's head. I'm convinced that 90 percent of the pent-up feelings were activated by the frustration of the group, in which the teacher tried to push others to express feelings they didn't feel. The only way a few kids were able to get themselves off the hook was to admit to feelings I'm sure they never had. Then they got a big hug and were left alone. No wonder we talk up and reveal whatever others are looking for. What a shuck. How is that very different from giving Miss Jones your best posture in the fourth grade when she walks by your desk so you can get a pat on the head?

Another more or less destructive assumption of the free school milieu is the idea that they are preparing children not for the society as it is, but for the society as it should be. The society as it should be is one of love, trust, acceptance, and unselfish giving. It is one where all men are equal, brothers, partners on the journey. Right on!

The problem lies in the process of bringing that about and the consequences to individuals for trying. I wonder, for example, if denying children the opportunity to compete with each other solves the problem of competition? I have good, humanistic friends who have spent a bit of time in India and just pray for the emergence of some dirty, capitalistic competition. The idea of letting everybody just do their own thing and avoiding issues of competition may be preparing a large group of people for ultimate starvation, or at least hard times which are not necessary for "beautiful" living. The problem is that these people conceive of competition as being intrinsically bad and leading to an invidious and destructive basis for interpersonal relations. This is not necessarily so. The problem is not the game but the rewards of it. In addition to our specific competitive failures, we are made to suffer for them. We do not know that to miss the ball, or run the slowest race, is not the same as failing as a person. Most cultures generate competition; many do it in pure fun. And it is unfortunate that our society leads us to believe that every time we compete it is the winning that counts rather than having a good time.

Sports can and should be fun, but I do not think that resorting to the notion that we all compete only with ourselves solves the basic problem. The confusion of this issue often leads free schoolers to rob kids of their right to enjoy many activities which their culture has taken a long time to perfect. In the absence of the ability to help children distinguish between personal failure and competition, we shuck out by eliminating competition all together.

One last note about competition, from the really old-fashioned cynical side. I have just learned that the Humanistic School Society is having its three-day conference on the same weekend the Open Schooling Fair is scheduled. Already one free school group is beginning to compete with another for the commitment of the membership. Before you know it, one school will be ripping off another school's kids, and the end to all of this is the inevitable shootout, organic vegetables at 20 yards.

Another assumption directly related to the issue of producing beautiful people (or, more appropriately for the current notion, letting them be themselves, which is beautiful) is the contention that beauty is what is natural. Many free schools see themselves as a natural environment. Free school people like to let their hair grow and fall naturally, raise organic fruits and vegetables, get close to animals, and let kids sit on the grass under the trees and be natural. Now I really don't want to play the role of cynic here, because we are dealing with very beautiful people, people I would gladly bring home for supper and whom I would trust with my kids, for a little while anyhow, because they really mean well.

But the idea that natural is best is really a very narrow perspective on the history of civilization. Hurricanes and earthquakes are natural, cancer and TB are natural, droughts and floods are natural; it is natural for animals to eat other animals and man when they can get at him. But culture and civilization have brought us to where we can control nature, and made it possible for a mass society to exist together. Nobody would argue that in the course of developing this civilization, many evil and stupid men have brought us to the verge of disaster and are still doing so. And I would agree that if the only way we can get rid of the dirty bath water is to give up the baby, let him go. But I do think it is possible to drain just the bath water and retain some of the benefits of culture. This is particularly possible in the area of schooling, but only if we accept the reality that natural is one thing and schooling another, and that the best possible way to overcome natural disaster is a very slightly "unnatural" schooling.

I often think that the big natural trip—like the back-to-craftsmanship trip, the astrology trip, the antiscience, antiinstitution, and antiteaching trips—is part of a grand plan to turn the most important sociocultural task, that of educating the young, over to rank amateurs. The true believers in destiny, intuition, and natural growth have suddenly discovered that hard work and rigorous training and the whole notion of expertise is a grand shuck, which it no doubt has become. Therefore, the opposite, the gut level reaction and the star track, can be legitimately substituted. It is at this point that I turn away from the apostles of the new order and establish myself as the worst form of enemy, the well-meaning liberal.

The thing I really question is why the kids and their parents have to pay all that money for natural, intuitive, organic education? Wouldn't it be cheaper to hire a couple of sheep herders and send the kids out to graze in all that good organic alfalfa? There is a place for discipline, application, and consideration for others. We are human beings after all, and consciousness is our own peculiar evolutionary burden. Perhaps it is time we learned to develop it in ways that counteract and balance egocentrism and animality among less responsible humans, many of whom control our lives.

Free schoolers, like counter culturists in other areas (for example, therapy, theater, and the arts) are able to pull their shucks in as baffling a vernacular as the establishment. On Madison Avenue, they'll shuck you with terms like "organizational development," "marketwise," "subliminal process," and the like. The behavioral scientists will blow your mind with "differential socialization," "reinforcement," "analytic models," "conceptual systems," and "paradigms." But how does that differ from "relate" and "feel" and "bump up against" and "turn on" and "heavy" and "tripping" and "relevant" and, above all, "meaningful"?

I went to a meeting of a group of people starting a free school and I asked the group (they don't acknowledge a leader) to tell me what they were going to do with my kid. They told me they would let her "do her own thing," "be herself," that they would "turn her on" to learning and help her "relate" to the group.

"Good," I said, "how are you going to do that?"

"Oh it just happens naturally."

"But suppose it doesn't happen?" I said, naively.

A sweet little woman about 19 put her hand on my leg and gave me a gentle smile which, if she wasn't counter culture I would have sworn was patronizing, and said "Just trust, my friend, just trust."

I suppose we do have to have trust, but not exclusively. I do want to know something about the people I trust. So I asked about who they were. How were they qualified?

Now, another way to shuck your way into getting people to trust you, other than the conventional ways we all put down, is to define yourself as being opposed to the evil other, without revealing your own thing at all.

One guy started out by saying, "Well, you know that we don't believe in credentials or degrees. We all know what they really stand for." Everybody nodded agreement. "I mean if you want degrees and credentials, well, that's what public schools are for. They can't *do* anything so they rely upon their college degrees and accreditation."

Another woman, mother earth herself, said "We are just human beings and I happen to think that's just the best thing anybody can be."

"Right on!" said the group.

"Isn't it enough to know we are not prisoners of a system? We can make things happen because a principal isn't telling us how to wear our pants and a superintendent is not telling him. Everybody just lets everybody be."

Earth mother said, "I've raised four children and not one has done well in public school. If they did, well, they just wouldn't be my kids."

"Right on!"

"We can all be teachers, and the children will teach each other, and we will teach each other. We are all parents and we are all children and we are all teachers."

Sure, I thought, then how come we don't pay the kids? That's just my Philadelphia cynicism showing up again. I'm really trying, but it's hard. So I kept pushing and asked, "But just as an example, tell me one thing you are going to do."

The 19 year old said, "We're just going to let the children be free and when they need us we'll be there. That's all you can do."

"But suppose they don't come?"

I know, we said it all together, "Just trust."

Having dealt with some of the major assumptions behind the free school movement, it is time to consider a little background. It is sometimes easier to detect a shuck when you know something about the history of the system to which the various educational policies owe allegiance.

A history of contemporary activities which we sometimes call "humanistic" or "liberating" can be traced to a few social-historical developments. The first would be the fact that we have evolved to an age of affluence. We have reached a period in our social progress when

(a) people have much leisure, (b) people have much money, (c) the children of people with both leisure and money aren't as motivated to strive for the same rewards as their parents once were (and probably still are).

Second, we have achieved the ultimate and logical goal of our industrial striving, for we have become a nation of specialists—so much so that we are pinched at both ends, in our industries, where our experts can't communicate with each other, and in our schools, where many of our brightest young people will no longer buy the unending chain of delays between them and human gratification. We know from almost universal reports how dehumanizing most professional schools are, for example. It is yet to be seen how many more young men, in a time of awareness of alternatives, are going to be able to accept the rigid way we are made into experts.

To attempt to alleviate the problem in industry, we have developed a way of making persons more aware and sensitive. Sensitivity training was intended primarily, in this way, to help organizations become even more efficient and productive. To handle the problem of extensive depersonalized training periods, those who are most aware are the dropouts. I think the important contribution these people have made to our history of consciousness is the simple demonstration that alternatives do exist. Not every middle-class Jewish boy has to become a professional and not every jock has to go into the FBI. But, to continue the mini-history of the free school consciousness, we now introduce such forces as divorce, women's liberation, civil liberties, the youth movement, and the rise of the growth movement.

First, I'll discuss divorce and one-parent families as a way of life. When I was a kid, there wasn't much divorce around. Nobody could afford it. It was tough enough to live as two together, but separately? No way. This was especially true since women were mothers and little else. In the depression there were few jobs for men, much less for women. (I describe this situation in the attitude of sociological observation rather than as to how I think it should have been.) Now, men can afford two families and women can afford to let their men go, mainly because they are economically more protected.

When women get divorced, they begin looking for ways in which to make up for all the growth they missed during those years they were doing everything they could to meet their husband's needs. The demand creates the supply. Along came all the legitimate and less legitimate therapists, with their marvelous ways to make a woman free and open and giving and trusting, etc. Part and parcel of these women's exposure to new ideas, new creativity, new therapy, is their consideration of alternative life styles. Their children's education becomes a more serious problem, not only because they begin to see schools for what they have always been, but also because they consider that, if they can't give their children a full-time father, the least they can do is be sure they get a human education.

The divorce syndrome, as common as it is today, is also a force in the lives of those who do not experience divorce. For every family breaking up, there's another going through agonies to try to stay together. These people are also led to try new ways of life. They seek new ideas, ask for professional help in evaluating their lives. They also, shocked out of their complacency by the discovery that one or the other partner, or perhaps a child, is very unhappy, begin to see things that were always there but were never noticed. I am talking about the availability of alternatives. Alternative ways of relating to each other, of living, and even, of schooling.

The second new force, women's liberation, should not be described by a man, but I must say something about it as it relates to my general theme, which is how people started thinking about alternative education. When women began insisting on their right to live fulfilling lives, which at times took them into the job market on a full-time basis, there was both more money and more interest in private schools. And, once a person decides a private school would be a good thing, he or she has earned the right to consider his or her options. When you start thinking about the kind of education you want to offer to your child, you have created an option, the possibility of an alternative.

Those women who began to ask questions about their roles as wives and mothers were ripe to be thinking about alternative education. The notion of alternatives is, I believe, a comprehensive idea, which coheres a large number of specific activities. The point is that once we are able to seriously question an institutional act we have always before taken for granted, then we are more likely to question all institutional acts. Any woman who can say maybe there is something for a woman to be other than a housewife and mother, is also capable of saying that maybe there is a way for a child to be educated other than in public schools.

Related to the liberation consciousness of women must be the important consideration that their inferior status and opportunities did not just happen. They were trained for it. And where were they trained for it? In the public schools. While it has not been a major theme of the book it should be mentioned that public education has always been sexist. Boys are taught to be boys and girls are taught to be girls and at critical points of differentiation one goes to carpentry and another to homemaking, and later one goes to medical school and one becomes a teacher. Now, if you were a mother just out of a bad marriage, trying to gain some balance and sense of worth and dignity, and looking around for people and places to blame, and if you had a daughter, would you send her to public school? The structure of education is sexist, it's alternative must not be. Unfortunately, my observation leads me to conclude that most free school types are pretty sexist also. At the picnic it is still the men playing ball and the women preparing the food.

Civil liberties are another consideration. It is not a far step from sitting in in Alabama to taking your kid out of public school. The struggle for civil liberties in this country, at least in modern times, was patterned by black people. Those who were denied the fundamental right to the same opportunities as others discovered that laws sometimes need to be challenged and changed. That entrenched patterns could be disrupted amazed most people. And the sympathy of those who understood restrictions and restraint in their own lives went out to the minorities. In the past quarter of a century we have challenged both authority and convention in areas of personal liberties and we find ourselves on the verge of victories in numerous areas: abortion, sexual freedom, marijuana smoking, and education. In the black community, primarily, the outcome of some effective techniques for opening up a racist system (riots, sit-ins) have led to alternative schools, run by community leaders. Some schools have emphasized black studies exclusively, others leaned more toward assuring that the children learn basic skills. The idea of the store-front school, paralleling the store-front church as a social institution, has gained popularity among radical educators of all races, basically as a way to build the notion of community as a potent force in both education and politics. Community schools, as political centers, operate on the notion that centralized education deprives both children and adults in economically deprived areas of a way to influence the type of education that goes on in their own schools.

Unfortunately, in my opinion, the viability of these schools has been threatened or closed out by the shuck politicians who, like "qualified" helpers everywhere, are willing to support people as long as they do what we want them to do. I understand that some mishandling of funds has occurred in some places, and that too derails the community school possibility. Between those who hold the purse strings and many who are trying to get a piece of the purse, the alternative school in the minority community is barely surviving. But at least it has provided us with the idea that decentralized, alternative, community-based education is possible.

Then we come to the youth movement. Young people everywhere find themselves confronted with the struggle to make their own world and, in the meantime, to live in the one already created in a way they feel is right. They have been constrained in every area of their lives, particularly in education. The men have faced the draft, often seeking education they don't want as a lesser of the two evils. The women have the pill on the one hand and their parents on the other. Sometimes the two are not incompatible, but usually they are. But postwar youth have also expanded beyond sex and compulsory nationalism; they have some sense of world community, of world citizenship. Nevertheless they are asked immediately upon entering adulthood to participate in a war they neither created nor can conscience. They must run from the prospect of killing third-world people, they must avoid the draft, they are rejected for their personal styles of hair and clothing, they are busted for smoking pot or congregating at rock concerts and antiwar marches, they are distrusted by businessmen, investigated and misunderstood by the power politicians, mistreated by teachers and professors, and despised by the police.

Now the major point I wish to make here is that youth not only have survived their struggles with entrenched conservatism, but that they are on the verge of prevailing. In the very best heroic tradition they have resisted what most of their parents have never resisted, the inalienable right to sell out. We offer them jobs, money, degrees, color TV's and wall-to-wall carpeting—things that many generations in a row have given everything to obtain. But for some reason they regard their souls as not for sale. From whom did they learn this? There were very few models in my time. All we have required of them is to cut their hair, wear better clothes, work hard in school, take nice jobs, marry nice other persons, give up those funny little cigarettes, and visit Mom and

Dad once a week (but call twice), and they can have it all. But they resist. Incomprehensible.

Many young people have made it apparent to me and others I know that there is more than one way to run a college class. And educators both in and out of the "system" are beginning to discover that there really is some significance in the word "relevance," even if the poor kids can't make sense of it for us, in our terms. One of the biggest and most dishonest shucks I know is the one that says these kids can't be worth listening to because they haven't come up with an alternative we can accept. They run them down for striking or dropping out or for forming their own living units and schools simply because they don't approve of their alternatives. Relevance can't be talked about in rationalistic terms the way efficiency experts can talk. Relevance can only refer to an individual's personal experience and his sensed understanding of the worth of things to him.

And that's part of the problem in the generation gap. Kids feel something their parents and teachers don't understand. Fortunately, enough parents are around who will support a school that intends to teach to that personal relevance, something old schoolers don't do.

A decade ago four musicians from Liverpool wrote a bunch of songs about truth and liberty and courage and taking risks. They came to this country and sang these songs and they wore their hair longer than we did and the amazing thing about the Beatles was that they were possible. By "possible," I mean we were ready for them. They did not transform our consciousness, they just gave us examples of how it was all possible. So when they sang their truths we were able to say "I can dig it." Or, if we were intellectuals, we would say that when we stop laughing at people who are different, we make it eminently possible for people really to be different.

Finally, there is a brief general history of the growth movement. The idea is basically simple. Growth is an internal matter. It happens inside a person and is unrelated to the evaluation of that person. That is, we don't grade spirituality or openness or trust or feeling good. By grade I mean the ongoing evaluation that takes place whenever people try to apply an objective or external standard to everyone they meet.

Once we understand and accept the notion that we as human beings should not make a habit of grading each other, we then begin to free each other to be unique, to really be individuals. But by that time it's already too late. Most of us over 20, perhaps 30, have spent too many years rejecting that way of thinking and developing strategies to do well in our everyday evaluations. We have trained ourselves to perform against external standards of what a man or woman, boy or girl, is supposed to be. We have had to look good, which means we never show our weakness; we perform well, which means never trying anything at which we might fail; we distrust everyone, which keeps us on guard against each other; and we hide our emotions because we don't want either to reveal too much or to be embarrassed.

What we have discovered about this process is that it requires enormous energy to guard yourself against ever being yourself. Sometimes we are at least brain-liberated enough to say that if we didn't need all that energy to protect ourselves we might be able to use it to grow.

So, before we can "grow," we must free ourselves from the over-utilization of protective strategies. We must become liberated from our need to be secure, to look good, to have status, to belong. Otherwise, there is no time or energy to turn inward, to begin working on strengths that support from within rather than seeking approval which supports from without. Thus, in historical terms, enters the growth movement; or in sociological terms, the group encounter movement; or in my terms, the group grope shuck.

Here is a shuck speech by an encounter group leader, a growth center director, perhaps even a yoga master or a Sufi. It is directed to a band of the faithful, the true believers to whom meaning just is.

My name is (blank). I will be your leader on this journey. Sometimes, yes, perhaps even oft times, I will be your follower. We are all leaders, we are all followers. I will give to you what it is that I have and you need and you will give to me what I need and together we will take the walk down that difficult yet marvelous road together.

Our job is to learn to reach out and touch, and by touching each other we will learn how to reach into ourselves. We cannot do it alone. It is a shared journey. There will be times when we will need to call out to each other in pain. Yes pain, it will come, surely it will come. And we need to face our pain, through each other, and soon our pain will be transformed into our joy. We begin with a scream of pain and end with a shout of joy.

But that is not to be right now. Our journey begins with a single step. Do not long for the end of the road or the pot of gold at the end of the rainbow. It is not there. It is in you, it is here now and has always been within you. We are only looking for the door to ourselves.

The rules of the journey are simple. Speak truth, experience your pain, say what you feel and just be. (Lifts head with giant smile.) Just be.

And so the groupies begin to be. They begin to feel. God! Do they begin to feel, and they touch and squeeze and cry and relate! It's really something. And in between, they attack each other as a way to get out their anger, and then they caress, as a way to get out their gentle feelings, and they cry for sadness and as they develop love and trust, the exposure becomes intense. Sometimes they even take off their clothes. Mostly they take off their psychic wraps. Then they go home and don't see each other until next Thursday at 7:30.

Some of the growth centers are flourishing. They are mostly in the business of part-time relief. The kind of relief that political radicals (groupies are cultural radicals) think of as siphoning off revolutionary energy. Five days a week you work as a bureaucrat and because you are becoming aware you suffer, but as long as you can get off to the woods every other weekend for group gropes or a touchie feelie, you can put up with it. I see it as the same old shuck psychiatrists have been pulling for years. Simply a more up-to-date version of the Beverly Hills retreat, affectionately referred to as "couch canyon."

Some of my best friends and acquaintances are deeply involved in the encounter or group movement. Mainly they are looking for freedom and awareness, but some are seeking more sex. Mostly, they want to be free from the constraints of culture and society. They want to rise above their socialization to raise their consciousness to a level of seeing society and culture as completely arbitrary. They wish to do this in order to feel good all the time, to be up, very up. Deep down I believe that they want *in* on some very mystical secrets that have been withheld from them by the sad fact of their mortality.

Most of them are upper-middle-class Caucasians with considerable leisure. They usually run in cliques, disdaining outsiders. (Sometimes they just feel sorry for us.) And they are high risk takers. Or perhaps I should have said they will risk anything to get high. They move from psychedelic drug to psychedelic drug, therapist to therapist, encounter group to encounter group, growth center to growth center, Zen master to Zen master, guru to guru, until they find the "right" one. They also try different religions, diets, exercises, and astrological forecasts. They are the modern version of *On the Road.*

They have had a considerable impact upon free school education. In their attempts to liberate everybody's spirit, they have often created a culture of dependent liberation. If you don't act like you're free, you've had it. They look at an unfree child like a high school counselor looks at the doctor's son who won't make it in college.

These, then, as I see it, are some of the roots of modern free school education. Many of the free school shucks are derived from shuck models in the growth movement. Some of them are done in jest, like the time I watched a class being organized, with officers and responsibilities, like passing out paper, in terms of birth signs. "OK, Mary, you're an Aquarius, you can be in charge of the poetry books. No, not collecting, just passing out. We need a Capricorn for gathering up."

Many are not in jest, for the thinking that allows us to assert we are teachers, without any formal training, is the same that permits us to assert that we are therapists, just because we are such loyal patients. I know some teachers, fresh from an encounter group weekend, who have returned to the classroom as sensitivity group leaders.

For example, a third-grade teacher might say: "All right class, today we are going to play some games that will help us understand ourselves better and help us relate to each other. Now let us all get in a big circle. Good. Now who shall we begin with? (Johnny raises his hand as do many others, ignorant of the task.) OK, Johnny, now what we will all do is go around the big circle and tell Johnny something we don't like about him."

The following day Johnny's mother comes to talk to the teacher and explains that Johnny has been crying for hours. The teacher explains how it is to give children feedback on their behavior, to improve interpersonal relations. The mother asks why the negative feedback wasn't balanced with positive feedback. The teacher responds that they did use positive feedback, but that was another exercise so somebody else had to be chosen. "After all, there are 35 kids in the class and they all want to be part of the game. We have to be fair."

Paradoxically, we have reached the age of amateurism at the same time we have entered into the age of the specialized expert. But this is not so unpredictable. Every period produces persons who react against the times. Periods of totalitarianism produce our best revolutionary writers. Amateurism is a predictable response to the smothering demoralization of a society of experts. Unfortunately, in its present form, it is probably just as dangerous, particularly when amateur therapists roam our children's classrooms unchecked.

Not that I believe amateur therapists do less good than trained experts. I'm not that reactionary. I just suspect that they might do more harm. Unfortunately, the free school movement is riddled with professional patients, teachers, and parents, none of whom make a move without consulting their therapists. This has produced an unfortunate consciousness which transforms a school into a giant couch and which is, I believe, as dangerous as the consciousness produced and maintained by self-righteous, rigid, public school teachers. We speak in the name of freedom and try to get a bunch of kids hung up on their navels. The shift is from rules to navels.

As I see it, there's no advantage. Freedom, in this sense, is the capacity to work between the rules and the psyche without being pathologically hung up on either. It is just as controlling to be dependent on seeing your mother as it is to be dependent on not seeing your mother. It is just as unfree to give in to external rules as it is not to give in. This doesn't mean one should or one shouldn't; it only means we should have a choice.

I want the children in my school, or the young adults in my classroom, to have the choice of meeting my expectations or meeting their own, or doing both. I think young children should have the choice of going to college or not going to college. They should understand that both choices are possible and that there is support for both. And so, in the name of giving them a choice, we have to prepare them for survival in both worlds. They have to be able to make leather belts as well as being able to do algebra. The free school shuck, at its worst, is the one that talks about freedom and choice and educates a child in such a way that he has no choice.

Many parents are beginning to suspect this, and while they like the free environment, they are beginning to suspect that such freedom, in the long run, removes freedom, as it removes choice. And so they withdraw their children from the free schools, and the free schools close, one after another. The failure rate is high, and will continue to be high until the beautiful amateurs and the well-meaning pros discover the means by which real freedom is possible. My own view is hopeful and despite my, at times, cynical treatment of the movement, quite supportive. The time has come when alternative educators must stop treating all of their criticism as the feeble ramblings of establishment educators. There is only one way to build viable alternatives in education, and that is with an eye to a wide range of considerations and concerns, even if these are made known by "professional" educators.

CHAPTER TEN

Conclusion

What I would like to try to get across in this last chapter is a conception of an alternative to shucking and a statement about some problems that keep us from moving on to alternatives. Let me begin with the second part first.

I think the reason why most atrocities, be they schools or the ways that people relate to each other, persist is because well-meaning people never understand that principles sometimes apply to them and that, if one wants changes, he may have to do something about producing them. The majority of Americans who have some sense about the basis of problems in our society don't do anything about them, not anything that counts anyhow. They may go to Mike Nichols movies and say "right on," but this act of liberal catharsis takes care of it all. Most of these well-meaning people who "understand" come to life every four years and go to the polls and vote for the least facist presidential candidate that they can find on the ballot. Or they send $15 a year to the American Civil Liberties Union and $10 to the NAACP and that's the end of it.

We have a similar situation with shucking. The majority of parents who read this book will agree with the major considerations. They will find shucks or worse in most of the conventional educational structures that I have discussed, but they will keep sending their kids to public schools, mainly on the grounds of "we can't afford a private school," "I want my child to go to school with his friends in the neighborhood," "Johnny is doing so well in school I wouldn't want to take him out," "I know that schools are generally bad but this year Mary has one of the best teachers in the school. Maybe next year."

The point is that we understand (we aware types) other peoples shucks but we can't for the moment detect our own. Of course there is good reason for not hearing our own shucks. If we did, we either would have to act or to feel guilty, and most of us can't handle either.

Let's look at our own shucks. First, we can't afford to send our kid to a private school. A private school costs about $100 a month, some more, some less. The biggest shuckers are those who have new cars every couple of years, $3000 or $4000 in the bank for a rainy day, a couple of insurance policies in case something happens to the breadwinner, and a vacation cottage on the beach or in the mountains. They are quite willing to lay out about $4000 a year to send their kids to college because that's required, and besides they get a payoff that they can see. But when it comes to an alternative to the big shuck that ruins their kid during the first 15 years of his or her life, they can't really see how it can be that important.

For people who really don't have any money, the options are fewer, but still possible. If I were poor and didn't have the opportunity to start my own school in my own neighborhood, I would get on public transportation and go around to every free school in the city and ask them to give my kid a scholarship. If I lived in the ghetto I would get every parent together and go in and take over my community school until it became a community school and not just a cool-out school, as are most ghetto schools.

Second, the "I want my kid to go to school with the other kids in the neighborhood" shuck. In America, we do not have communities, we have geographical areas filled with competitive individuals, both children and adults. Before the age of nine or ten these so called "communities" provide children with other bodies to keep busy with but friends are collected and cast off at such regular intervals that most kids couldn't care less if they move. The sad irony of this shuck is that parents never let it stand in the way when they are ready to "move to a better neighborhood."

If it is just bodies that count then any neighborhood will do and if it's maintaining continuity for friendship between neighborhood and school then we have two questions, "What does it matter?" and "What is a friend?" I really don't know why it is important to go to school with a friend. It certainly can't mean that friends are useful to a student during the school experience, since most conventional schools provide very little basis for interaction. Actually, the way most teachers run classrooms, if you have a friend you're more likely to get into trouble, since you are more apt to talk when you're not supposed to than if your friend wasn't there.

Or perhaps a friend is to be defined as someone to help you, and vice versa, over the hardships of public education, someone to sit around with after school and share your hatreds of teachers and school activities—kind of a misery-likes-company theory. Of course if the kid didn't go to that kind of school he wouldn't need anybody to share his misery.

What does it really matter whether a kid goes to school with a friend or makes a friend in school whom he brings home from another neighborhood? The neighborhood excuse is both a shuck and the beginning of a great danger of consciousness. It leads us into centering our identity within a geographical unit. Sooner or later we end up defending this unit against other geographical units, or protecting ourselves against the invasion of people unlike ourselves with ideas unlike ours. The long-range consequence of this kind of thinking, when looked at in terms of cities, states, and nations, should be obvious.

There is also nothing to say that children who go to school out of the neighborhood lose their friends in the neighborhood. The argument is both weak and trivial. Let's move on.

What about the proposition that says that when a student is doing well in the neighborhood school it is no time to take him out. Nonsense: This is all the more reason to get him out immediately. Passive kids do very well in public school, and their passivity is reinforced everywhere they turn. But perhaps doing well means something else, like getting along or getting A's on tests. Public schools, as we know, are not organized to help kids get along. If they seem to be getting along it probably means that they are meeting everybody's expectations. But getting along should mean getting along within a framework of individual differences. Schools are organized to present students with a rule model of everyday deportment that reduces stress for teachers and administrators. Interpersonal freedom is not possible in monolithic structures ruled from such high places that children never even get to see the people who make the rules. So getting along comes to mean finding a way to fit in. Why would we want our children to fit in to something in which we don't believe? What is more important to us—our values and beliefs about human rights and dignity, or fitting in?

If "doing well" means getting good grades then the kid is really in trouble, especially if the grades become important to him. And if this hasn't been made clear by the content of this book, then nothing has. But if we understand the destructive long-range consequences of getting hung up on grades then it is clear that we cannot permit this to happen to our children.

What else can doing well mean? Perhaps we are talking about a child who has been insecure and frightened but is now beginning to show some confidence, some self-assurance. All I can say is that if this change was a consequence of public education then I would distrust the foundation of the confidence. Perhaps the confidence comes at the point that the child feels he can compete with the others. That is wonderful, isn't it? He is now transformed into a child who is ready to fight the good fight on everybody else's battlefield but his own.

Finally, the matter of the fortuitous circumstance that made it possible for one's child to have a really good teacher. Now, does this imply that a really good teacher is a really good teacher anywhere or just that, given what we can expect of public school teachers, this one is exceptional? In my terms a really good teacher is one that would have a hard time in public schools. If a good teacher did exist, he or she would be in trouble most of the time, and probably would be shipped to a school where he or she couldn't do too much harm. But since suburban schools are in suburban communities and since I am talking about suburban-type parents, it isn't likely that rebels would survive for very long in these schools. Granting that one did survive, are we really talking about an alternative to the shucking structure? Are we talking about a teacher who doesn't invoke rules about talking or leaving your seat? Are we talking about a teacher who allows children to construct their own course of study and constructively provides them with resources? Are we talking about a teacher who does not give tests which lead to invidious evaluations of children? Are we talking about a teacher who fights for the right not to give grades? What really are we talking about when we make a decision to keep our children tied to an inhuman system of training and socialization?

Are we building a case in defense of our inability to act in our children's best interest or a case which argues that we *are* acting in our children's best interest? My contention is that it is almost always the former. The shuck comes in when we argue that it is the latter.

The sad state of public education today is only possible with the full cooperation of shucking parents, in the same sense that the sad state of human relations in the country is fully a consequence of blind self-interest on the one hand and the inability to act on the other. The quiet, silent, uninvolved American has been lauded by many political elites, as well he should be, for it is his uninvolvement in the affairs of his country, state, city, and neighborhood that makes it possible to maintain the status quo in the best interests of those who run it all.

That roughly describes the parent's consciousness, the basis on which he or she is unable to see the relevancy of acting in his or her own life. Now, how do we account for the teachers' problem of consciousness? Why are they unable to be different? Or perhaps we might ask more fundamentally, what rationale do teachers use to excuse their inability to act in ways that they know would be better, both for themselves and for the children?

If a teacher understands the basis of his or her own alienation, the teacher will likely say, "The system is too big and I am only one person," or "It is better to stay here and do what little I can than be fired and do nothing," or "When I get to be an administrator I can do something and radicals don't get to be administrators," or "I just can't afford not to have the job," or, and this one I find to be most prominent, "When I close my door nobody knows but me and the students what goes on behind it." The implication of this last is that the teacher is doing all sorts of radical and exciting things behind not only the door but also the backs of administrators, and maybe parents.

Let's look at the first shuck, "There's only little old me to fight that whole big monster." The thing I have never been able to fathom is why we perpetuate myths that we never observe in our own lives. Why is the

David and Goliath story so admired when what we really mean is "That little David was a fool to pick up a stone against that giant." The basic concept of heroism in our culture is founded upon the notion of fighting against heavy odds, particularly when, and perhaps only if, the cause is worthy. Why is it that nobody wants to be a hero?

How are problems to be solved if nobody wants to take a stand against the forces that create those problems? Sometimes, believe it or not, the changes we are so afraid to make will not be so seriously resisted by those who have the authority to authorize changes, if only on an experimental basis. The cry that the forces of opposition are too imposing is often a preliminary rationalization for our basic reluctance to stand up for what we believe in anywhere. Children are trained to be passive, to conform, not to stand up for their differences, even though we say we applaud individualism and courage. That's another shuck isn't it? I have sometimes found in my own career that standing up for something was not always rewarded by a sense of heroism. Sometimes I got what I wanted without striking a single blow or receiving one. What a disappointment when you're all set to become a martyr.

Suppose things should go the way we most expect. I would be the last one to encourage people to act on the grounds that they might succeed. I have to be realistic and argue that failure can and should be expected. Again, our earlier training paralyzes us. We are conditioned against failure, as if failure somehow defeats us as persons. And yet our cultural heroes are often failures. The act of heroism doesn't involve winning, only acting courageously in behalf of a worthy cause. What we need, in the long run is an educational alternative that helps children understand that accepting the possibility of failure removes from one the fear of trying new and difficult things. But to bring this educational alternative into existence some teachers somewhere are going to have to act as models. Who among us is the Joan of Arc of the Classroom?

Next is the "At least I'm doing something" shuck. One way that something can be seen to be a shuck is when it is obvious that the alternative is never juxtaposed seriously against the decision. Is it better to stay in and do something or to get fired and not be able to do that something? Teachers have been making this statement for a couple of decades. They really think they are doing a little something to humanize education, at least in their own personal contact with students. There are two problems, or at least questions that these teachers need to consider.

(1) How does this affect the overall picture in education? (2) How are those children we humanize in our own classes affected by their exposure to us when the rest of the time they are exposed to *them*.

The first is easy to answer—not very much. Education in this country is institutionalized, which is to say preset beyond the intervention of persons on an individual basis. The only way to affect persons differently than the institutional life now does is to institutionally change the patterns or structures. It is one thing to say nice things to a kid after you've given him a C. It is another to change the grading system. The best we can do without affecting the structures that depersonalize schooling is act as minor wet nurses, temporary balms for the tortured souls of students.

The second question asks: what is the consequence to students of personalizing part of the schooling experience while leaving the larger segment untouched? The answer: very disturbing for some, a relief for most. Students treat the humanistic classroom as a welcome relief to their ordeals in other kinds of classes. In self-contained classrooms students can have a good year which is followed by one that they consider routine or normal. Should students ever get the serious idea that school not only can, but should be fun, that's trouble. The question we humanistic teachers need to ask ourselves is "Are we opening them up too much for disturbing letdowns?" It may be if we force students to question the routines of study that they have used so successfully in the past, they won't do as well in their other classes.

I don't know the answer to this last question but most of the teachers who opt for humanizing their own classes a little bit don't have the answers either, and probably don't want them. The conclusion may require more drastic action. For if it is true that we don't make a difference in our small ways then we have to face the fact that we either have to do the big thing or admit to personal weakness—either way, a lousy choice.

Then there's the "when I get to be in a position of authority" shuck. This is a delaying tactic, one that most of us who were born and raised in a bureaucratic world well understand. It's the old copping out as a means to get to a place where we won't cop out game. It is means-to-an-end thinking in a stepladder world, where every rung is simply a step to the next rung. Most of us treat this consciousness as a way of life from birth to death. We are always doing something to get into a position to do something. Unfortunately, there's always one more rung to climb before we get into that proper position of authority.

We begin this kind of shucking in school and continue out in the job world. I've spoken to a lot of teachers who want to be administrators and they know that in order to move up you have to keep your nose to the grindstone and close to the rule book. Then when they become vice-principals they set their sights on the next rung. Only the top man in the educational bureaucracy has the final say and he's controlled in turn by the Board of Education who is responsive to the public through the city council or board of supervisors. It's a stranglehold system which, in effect, permits no one at any of the stratified positions to act purely from conscience or self. If anyone feels the need to act in an integrated manner, with self, he might as well do it right off rather than adding many cop out years to an already sold-down-the-river educational life.

I believe that deep down in every shucker's private awareness is the realization that what I am saying is true, but if one should believe it the consequence is terrible. We have to be ourselves before we're ready. We have to stand up for what we believe without any training to do so, or even very much chance to get ready. We really think that we need the bulk of our educational and professional life as a preparation for that one heroic act that we see every night on TV. Pathetically, we never get the chance. Because, believe it or not, a life of copping out does not prepare one for heroism, any more than a life of leisure prepares us for our great act of strength.

Many teachers feel that they really need the job, and I have no argument with those who really do. I have never been in a position to choose between starvation or copping out. The real shuckers in this category are those who don't differentiate between need and like. It's one thing to need the income. It's another to like it because of the extras it brings. I am talking mainly about those women who are supplements to a husband's decent income. What I have seen, however, in a female-dominated occupation, is a predominance of males who are willing to put their jobs on the line by becoming activists, particularly in union activities.

I do not want to juxtapose teachers against businessmen. By calling for teachers to act with integrity thereby endangering their careers is to ask them to accept an even wider disparity between their economic opportunities and that of businessmen. We are already too far behind. What must occur is not possible in a money-dominated society. We would have to think of teaching then as a consummate sacrifice which it should never be. The price of changing institutions cannot be calculated fairly in dollars and cents terms. The price of changing education in this country is so exorbitant in terms of sacrifice that the only thing that will ever do it is a dramatic shift in consciousness of present and future educators such that not earning a living is no big thing. This would require a sharing society and not an economically private one. It would require those who wish to teach in free schools either to get money from friends or to join together with others who feel the same way and set up a self-contained living as well as educational unit. Our small acts of caring about school kids are not paying off. We are running out of both time and money and we are too feeble as human beings to take the action that is required to save education in this country. This does not mean that some people in some places will not make important changes for some kids and for themselves. We do have an image of an alternative and some will have the courage to struggle through the gestation period of bringing this alternative to birth. But most of those who have the image do not have the courage. Why should they be expected to? Where would it come from?

The final rationale for inaction is the notion that we can disguise our good works behind closed doors, and even though we may act like we are going along with administrators we are really protecting the children from the consequence of their administration. Again I say it is not enough to improve our own little sector when we shall surely go down the drain with the rest of schooling when the deluge comes. The argument is age old. Do we plug up the old dike or construct a new one? It is an issue too involved to resolve here. All that I wish to question at this point is the possibility that persons find the answers that they personally need to rationalize their own inability to act against the organization as a whole. Most of my students who are completing a credential in teaching are absolutely certain that one can work within the established system and accomplish humanistic goals. And even when you present them with a strong argument against that possibility they hold to their belief. They do not have reasons, only feelings. They know that they are right; its just that I have so much more verbal ability than they do that makes my argument seem persuasive and theirs weak. I contend that, as a group, they are committed to a belief by their personal investment in time, money, and energy. If after all they are wrong, they have wasted a couple of years in preparation; therefore they are right by nature of energy expended. They are shucking themselves and each other and they have a mutual stake in each others shucks. They have attained the absolute opposite of the best intentions of an education, and they have done so at the conclusion of their formal training. They have come up with a closed mind.

From here on, I will be very specific, and not very cynical. When I talk about an alternative I am not talking the old tear it down game. I am talking very specifically of alternatives in structures or patterns that make public education what it is today. These are the structures that require the shucks. Without them there would be no need to pull a shuck, since shucks are only possible when people need to convince others that something in their worst interest is in their best interest. If we can argue that the alternative to shuck education is in the best interests of human beings both as individuals and collectively, then shucking is irrelevant. If, however, we continue to believe that conventional education is in the best interest of human beings, then what I have been arguing must be the opposite. I am either wrong, misguided, misled, etc., or I am pulling a shuck. But to argue that I am pulling a shuck would require that you describe the advantage that I derive from it. Of course, I get a book out of it; all possibilities exist. It's your decision.

Underlying much of what has been stressed in this book is a version of society as achievement oriented toward objective symbols of success. It is because, and only because we have come to value money and position and luxuries that we are willing to tolerate the rituals and frustrating educational routines that lead us in the "right" direction. Social mobility, as a way of life, pits human beings against each other in a striving competitive arrangement with consensus rewards at the finish line. By consensus rewards I am referring to the fact that things are valuable by definition, not by intrinsic nature. A new car is worth something because it is collectively valued by a social group. A degree is valued over knowledge or wisdom because a degree, like an income level, is a symbol, or a title like vice-president of the bank.

American society, as an achievement-ordered society has objectified reality to a point where subjective truths have become almost irrelevant. How one feels about something doesn't matter much. How one observably performs is paramount. Out of this focus on concrete objective reality has evolved a consciousness that puts us in constant danger of losing the world as a price of winning a collectively valued prize. And if we have been trained to lose our souls we can look to our major institutions as the training ground for our personal failures as human beings. The school of the objective consciousness should be known by all of us, for it is clearly within those structures that our human possibilities are determined.

The consciousness which accounts for our massive gross national product is also at the base of our schooling. It could be no other way. Institutions train human beings who are expected to maintain the objective consciousness in years to come. The following characteristics of our typical educational structures may thus be seen as logical outgrowths of our efficiency model of social life:

1. *Compulsory education.* If society wishes to maintain its control over the form of consciousness that exists, all persons must be socialized to see the world in that particular way.

2. *Bureaucracy.* Educational institutions are managed by persons in differentiated positions of power and authority. These positions are hierarchically arranged and contain the structure of power, independent of the individuals who may hold those positions.

3. *Universalism.* All students are evaluated against the same standard or standards. It is more efficient to develop a value which requires persons to compete for differential rewards than to reward individuals differently, based upon standards which suit the variety of responses possible in human life.

4. *Unidimensionalism.* Not only are all students evaluated against the same standard in all activities, the only evaluation that really counts is achievement. Other varieties of performance, such as creativity or curiosity are irrelevant to the allocation structure.

5. *Certification.* Education has established itself as a certification agency; persons receive credentials which communicate that they are a completed product of some course of study.

6. *Product-centeredness.* Education is organized with a view to the outcome or product. It is easier to assess one's means and whether or not one's goals have been met when outcomes are

clear and behaviorally specified. Focus upon the process would make it difficult to distinguish one product from another.

7. *Time and space-centeredness.* Persons are more efficiently locomoted to desirable outcomes when control can be exerted over the time and space allocated for educational activities. Evaluation can also be more efficient, since we know the time and space input more accurately. Linear consciousness requires persons to view progress as a series of steps separated by artificial landmarks (periods, semesters).

8. *Mass production.* Industrial consciousness has made its impact on education in the area of division of labor and responsibility for moving products along the educational conveyor belt in large units.

9. *Segregation.* Students are segregated by ability and sex, by rule and by race, and by economic status. Some interaction takes place by chance across categories, and the regularities of peer socialization occur primarily on a homogeneous base.

10. *Occupation-based.* Education is linked to the occupational structure in regular ways. Success in school predicts the level of probable occupational status.

11. *Centralization.* Control over educational process is maximized when decision making originates at the top and filters down to local schools in the form of orders. This makes variability less likely and community or individual influence less possible.

12. *Private identity.* Educational experiences are primarily individual and attainment the private possession of separate individuals. Statuses, in this way, are distributed along dimensions of private identity (my grades, my popularity, my participation scores.) The institution is itself private insofar as there is ordinarily only token interaction or cooperation with other agencies.

13. *Comprehensiveness.* All formal education is contained within the walls of the school. Other social agencies are prevented from certifying educational forms.

These structures constitute the organized implementation of a consciousness which relies upon efficiency as process, socially valuing rewards as "product." The fact that schools require attendance ensures a wide base for enculturation. Stratified positions ensure increased efficiency and encourage the striving for upward mobility. Universalism ensures a base of competition and, therefore, motivation for conformity and mobility. Unidimensionalism enables us to hold the line in the forms of competition we allow, thereby restricting mobility patterns to those who feed into the industrial-occupational structure. Certification gives us control over the mobility structure. Product-centered education maintains the industrial consciousness; if students came simply to enjoy the experience of education, without turning anything out, we could neither differentiate them or produce a product-oriented child. In fact, every item can be elaborated upon in such a way as to demonstrate its relationship to the objective consciousness. And, like other social structures, educational patterns depend on a wide base of ideological support to ensure their stability. In some areas, this support is not as available as in other times and places, for at the same time competing ideologies are emerging within the society, the public base of economic support for education is disappearing. The free school movement has benefited from both trends.

The support for an alternative to the structures outlined above comes from different directions and from people who seek diametrically opposed advantages from alternative schools. In minority communities the most prevalent parental concern is that the children receive an improved education so they can better compete for the rewards of the system. The parents want their children in the establishment and particularly in positions of influence and affluence. Free schools are also being generated among the disaffected middle classes, those who have attempted to discover some alternative to the life style imposed by the technocracy. These are persons, mainly young adults, who are walking away from the affluent styles of their parents, who do not want their children exposed to the same education they received. Often these are parents who are sensitive to the problems of public education and are unwilling, due to their own shifted consciousness, to allow their children to be manipulated by the structures of the schools of the objective consciousness. These parents, or so it would seem, accept the notion that the child will learn what he wants when he wants as an alternative to the rule of the objective consciousness: the child will learn what we want him to learn when we want him to learn it. Behind this simplistic comparison lies an even more sophisticated pair of educational models which influence both what goes on in schooling and what goes on in higher education in the area of research and evaluation on schooling. We will turn to these models in a moment, but first a final word about the polarities of consciousness.

The school, in some senses, exists as a conventional structure because it has always existed in that particular way. As long as a society continues to operate along the lines of traditional values and reward structures, there would not be any reason to reject the presence of one of the major institutions that maintains these values and structures in stable equilibrium. On the other hand, if those values and reward structures lose their importance in social consciousness, then the function of schools is no longer clear, and it may then be necessary to consider alternatives to schooling. Illich speaks at length on this matter, suggesting the possibility (implying the desirability) of deschooling society and shifting desirable functions such as socialization and skill training to other social units. Illich's plan assumes that deschooling increases in possibility as conventional considerations, such as school financing and job market opportunities, become problematic. The value of deschooling, as interpreted by counter culturists, lies in the fact that it defeats the invidious consequences of what Illich calls the "hidden curriculum," and what sociologists would label the latent functions of the school—that is, the business of certification and the process of differentiation and segregation based upon race and economic status.*

A consciousness, is a conception of how one uses the society, in particular its major institutions, in order to attain the values one has developed. As we shift to the notion of alternative models of schooling, we need to emphasize the relationship of each model to the particular version of society on which it is founded. I have discussed in some detail the process of reward striving and the way in which conventional educational structures support the socialized need of persons to achieve concrete ends. I have emphasized the external or objectified state of goals and implied that a dependent relationship develops between persons and certain conceptual areas, like status and security, which these goals symbolize. I have also raised the issue of how an efficiency model of industrial functioning has provided the prototype for all institutional processes, and have suggested that this version of schooling analogically sees the child as a product comparable to a new car.

Putting all of this in schooling terms, we evolve a model of efficien-

*Ivan Illich, *Deschooling Society,*

cy, or achievement education linked to long-range symbolic rewards. Juxtaposed against this, and founded upon an alternative consciousness, emerges the personal growth or awareness model of schooling. The following chart reveals the comparison.

ATTENTION
AWARENESS

Humanistic Education	*Achievement Education*
Subjective (Means, Ends the same)	Objective (Means to ends)
Personal Interpersonal	Personal Interpersonal
Learning as growth	Learning as achievement
Motivation as awareness of need to grow	Motivation as social success
Teacher's task: make aware and facilitate growth	Teacher's task: provide tools for success

The two models begin by asking their respective students to pay attention, to become aware, on the one side to the self, and on the other to the objective rules. As we proceed down the left we will refer to HE or Humanistic Education. As we go down the right we will refer to AE, Achievement Education. On the HE track, one asks children to tune in to their being, all their feeling and thinking, and to what it is they need to do, or need to do next. On the AE tract, children tune in to the rules by which they are to play the game of education. They learn the means of achieving certain rewards which we also teach them to esteem, and how these means are to be expressed in behavior. In HE, however, they might discover that their own personal cues and behavior are the only directives for educational progress. Learning to learn becomes the means and the end.

Now, pushing on, we come to a distinction between personal and interpersonal awareness. For HE there is awareness of the self and its capacities and needs, and on the other, awareness of others. Others exist in the world and they relate to me in specific ways. They also relate to me in terms of feelings I have about them. Depending on which track we are on, the personal and interpersonal dimensions of awareness have very different meanings. In the AE track, we become aware of ourselves in relation to expectations and rules for achieving. We become aware of others in similar terms; that is, we center on what others mean to us in terms of helping or retarding our progress toward desirable goals. Hence, we engage in competition with classmates and compliance with teacher. On the HE track, the personal awareness motif translates into a matter of consulting oneself and supposedly enjoying one's capacity to discriminate and sense the world. Awareness of interpersonal relations has to do with enjoying what others have to give and defining oneself in relation to others. That is, to experience who I am by discovering who I am not. The thinking is that we can only encounter ourselves in the context of others who are not us. Relations with others becomes a matter of defining ourselves rather than perceiving and meeting the expectations of others.

Then we come to a conception of learning. On the HE track, learning is defined by the growth that occurs regardless of how it is measured. On the AE track, learning is teacher defined, and objective defined, in terms of some standard or criteria of achievement which usually is in relation to our classmates.

Then, we have a conception of the teacher on each of these tracks. On the HE track, the teacher's task is to provide the children with experiences which improve their capacity to be aware of themselves and others and to develop their own unique potential. On the AE track, the teacher's function is to provide children with the cognitive and moral skills or habits necessary to succeed in a competitive society.

In the classroom, the achievement teacher routinizes activities and controls persons in line with his or her version of the teacher's function, which usually means getting kids to read and write and be polite. The HE teacher, by suggesting a more flexible and diverse range of learning experiences, intends to help the child become more aware of what he wants himself to be or do at any given moment, and facilitates learning and development in those directions.

I have concluded my cynical treatment of schooling in America with a more serious analysis of the specific issues underlying the problems that I have chosen to describe. As the reader has surely detected throughout, the shuck while usually portrayed as a humorous, sometimes silly process of interpersonal functioning, represents a deadly serious disjuncture in human affairs. I felt that some readers might like the opportunity to have all of my implications summarized in descriptive terms, even if I am forced to resort to academic writing. For this to some I apologize. Unfortunately everyday, ordinary life cannot be talked about in everyday ordinary language. It can only be experienced as it is. Once we stop to describe it we have to appeal to some convention of description or analysis. We could be philosophical, sociological, or psychological. Whatever we were we would not make too much sense to too many people. It is for this reason that intellectuals are usually impotent in real life affairs. And because the power elite in this country well understands this they do not fear the universities, for college professors cannot make sense of the real world without resorting to the rhetoric and grammar of their special disciplines and the frameworks these disciplines impose upon reality.

No, shucking must be described as experience, and only in addition analyzed as structure. It was my own particular need to which I yielded in the end to speak to those who need some formal framework for making sense of the world of impressions. Schools and schooling are everyday experiences and the amount of shucking that goes on is mind boggling. It may not matter much that one cannot talk about the structure and function of shucking but it surely helps to know that we're part of the game, because only then do we have what few students in this country are ever given—a choice to get out.